Dear Carer,

Sarah Martin

Published by Sarah Martin

NATIONAL LIBRARY OF AUSTRALIA

A catalogue record for this book is available from the National Library of Australia

Cover design by Hazel Lam

Edited by Kathryn Tafra

Printed by Ingram Spark

ISBN print 978-0-6456449-0-6

ISBN ebook 978-0-6456449-8-2

Formatted with Vellum

Our world is full of colour,
shades of black,
shades of white,
and times when there are lots of scribbles muddling it all up.

Love - steady, imperfect, or determined, can light even the darkest moments.

For carers,
this book is for you.

Sensitive content warning

This book contains sensitive content that may cause an emotional response. Sensitive content includes mention of self-harm, suicide, eating disorders and other topics that may cause distress. If you are in Australia and require support, please contact one of the services below:

Emergency Services 000
Lifeline 13 11 14 (24/7) or text 0477 131 114. Lifeline is a free 24/7 telephone crisis support service.
Suicide callback service 1300 659 467 (24/7)
Kids Helpline 1800 55 1800. Free confidential counselling by phone or web chat for 12–25-year-olds.
13Yarn 13 92 76. 13Yarn is a free 24/7 Aboriginal and Torres Strait Islander crisis support.
QLife 1800 184 527. Peer support from 3pm–midnight for LGBTQIA+ people.
Transcultural Mental Health Line 1800 648 911

Contents

What is mental health?

Understanding mental health: definitions and diagnostic tools

Mental health refers to a state of mental wellbeing.

In essence, good mental health allows individuals to manage daily stressors and negative emotional reactions while they deal with everyday activities, such as work, sport, school and other situations. Mental ill-health refers to periods where individuals are not able to manage daily tasks due to their psychological and/or emotional state.

In medical settings, illnesses such as schizophrenia, bipolar I and II, anorexia, and schizoaffective disorder are referred to as 'psychiatric conditions'. This may sound scary, but it is the language that doctors, nurses and allied health care teams use.

An alternative term is 'complex mental health concerns or conditions'. In *Dear Carer,* this is the term that will be used.

How is mental health defined in Australia?

Early care is when we might first hear the terms 'Mental Health Act', the '*Diagnostic and Statistical Manual of Mental Disorders* (DSM-5)', and 'International Classification of Diseases ICD-11 (known as the ICD-11)'. It's worth knowing a little about them.

Mental health legislation

I was surprised to find that mental health legislation in Australia varies from state to state. I went down a rabbit hole with this, so I will keep it brief.

If you are unsure of your rights and responsibilities in the mental health space, it is important to ask for documentation of local mental health legislation from your hospital. This can clarify how your loved one may be treated. There should be documentation at hand that will explain what your state's approach is regarding appropriate treatment and safeguarding your loved one's rights.

Each Australian state and territory has mental health legislation – a legal framework for the treatment, care, and rights of individuals with psychiatric conditions and mental health concerns. For example, in Victoria the act is called the *Mental Health and Wellbeing Act* 2022 (*Vic*); other states and countries use different words to describe their legislation. These acts protect patients' rights and serve to keep them safe while they receive the correct care and treatment.

Some basic definitions are listed below but please clarify your state or countries legislation (see 'Links to Resources' section).

Involuntary treatment orders: these orders require individuals to be detained in a mental health facility for treatment.
Patient rights: the right to be informed about treatment and care.
Emergency provisions: if a person's mental ill-health causes harm to themselves or others, police or paramedics can authorise emergency transport to the hospital for assessment.

Consumer involvement: notes the importance of involving patients and their support person or carer in a treatment plan. The patient (or 'consumer') holds the right to consent to treatments; a carer or guardian may consent on the behalf of those involuntarily admitted.

REMEMBER: Legislation varies from state to state and between countries.

Check your state (or country's) legislation.

Each state's legislation can be looked up online. There are user-friendly guides and resources to help you interpret and understand your rights and responsibilities.

What are the DSM-5 and ICD-11?

These are the primary diagnostic manuals used within Australia's medical system.

DSM is the acronym for the *Diagnostic and Statistical Manual of Mental Disorders*. DSM-5 refers to the most recent (fifth) edition. It provides a list of mental disorders and focuses on symptoms and treatments. ICD-11 is the acronym for International Classification of Diseases – an international standard maintained by the World Health Organisation. The ICD-11 is used for the study of disease distribution, patterns in the population and determinable factors.

The DSM-5 is used by many psychiatrists, doctors and psychologists in diagnosing psychiatric conditions. Some use the ICD-11 as an alternative or in conjunction with the DSM-5.

You may never hear your medical team talk about the DSM-5 or the ICD-11, but it is good to be aware of these acronyms – it can be confusing and disheartening when acronyms are used and you do not understand what they are.

Chapter 1
Why did I write Dear Carer?

> Carers are our parents, siblings, friends, colleagues, and the multitude of others that may sit next to us on the bus, in a chair at the emergency department, or those that care for our loved ones in hospital. Mental ill-health does not discriminate.
>
> — Sarah

I've been told to never start a book with statistics but this book is all about breaking the stigma and silence of mental health concerns, advocating for our loved ones and ultimately ourselves, so, where else to put them but at the start?

In Australia there are over three million unpaid carers. Nearly one million of that number care for those living with complex mental health concerns.[1] In fact, the Australian Bureau of Statistics states

1. https://www.carersaustralia.com.au/wp-content/uploads/2024/10/Final-CWS-2024-Report-compressed.pdf Source 2023 Regional Wellbeing Survey, November 2023-March 2024

that, in a 2020–2022 study, '42.9% of people aged 16–85 years had experienced a mental disorder at some time in their life.'[2]

The population of Australia in 2022 was twenty-six million ... ish. That's over eleven million people who had experienced mental health concerns or conditions. In September 2025, the World Health Organisation released an article stating one billion people around the world were living with mental health conditions.[3]

Who is looking after those living with complex mental health concerns and conditions?

We know who it is. It's us.

Carers can be parents, siblings, friends, colleagues, and a multitude of others. They may sit next to us on the bus or in a chair at the emergency department, or they may be one of those who care for our loved ones in hospital. Mental ill-health does not discriminate; anyone can be called upon to care for a loved one.

Regardless of how complex mental health concerns entered your life, life has changed. The tentacles of mental ill-health touch all who take part in caring, loving, or living with you. They can also reach friends and family who can see and hear what's happening in your world.

The dramatic representations of complex mental health conditions that we might see in the media are a sad reality for some, but they are not the norm. Recovery is often painstakingly slow and quiet – it may go unseen by many. But carers see the whole process. We also see the stigma, shame, and misperceptions that surround complex mental health conditions.

And these, my dear friends, are some of the reasons why many of

---

2. www.abs.gov.au/statistics/health/mental-health Released 5/10/2023
3. www.who.int/news/item/02-09-2025-over-a-billion-people-living-with-mental-health-conditions-services-require-urgent-scale-up September 2025

us do not share our mental health stories. My mission is to change this narrative.

As well as the very real challenges, mental health concerns can also bring laughter, joy, and love. It's not all doom and gloom, especially if we have support from family, friends and medical personnel. We can develop a toolkit of knowledge and establish a plan of action for when our loved ones are ill – led by and developed in collaboration with them.

In 2015, mental ill-health walked in our front door uninvited. We stayed silent because of stigma, grief, and the unknown.

Our twenty-one-year-old daughter was on the journey of a lifetime. A coming-of-age adventure that she had worked hard for. Three months into her trip, on a beautiful Saturday morning in August, I received a message from a stranger, who was concerned that she was experiencing some sort of mental health crisis.

We live in Australia. Our girl was in Istanbul, Türkiye. Her guardian angels – Syrian refugees, friends that she had met five short weeks before – kept her alive and safe until my oldest son and I could get there. It was clear upon our arrival that she was very unwell – hearing voices, not one but hundreds. She was in the grip of psychosis; our girl needed psychiatric care, and urgently.

After an exhausting 28,000km round trip, we arrived back in Australia. Her reality differed from ours. She had no perception that what we saw and heard was different to what she saw and heard. And we had no insight into what was going on in her brain, other than knowing it was misfiring in all directions.

When we arrived at the emergency department, we had to tell our story to six different doctors and nurses in three hours. The triage nurse, junior doctor, admission nurse, registrar, mental health nurse, and finally the psychiatric registrar. Seven hours later, our daughter was 'scheduled' and involuntarily admitted into the psychiatric emergency care centre (PECC), which provides urgent care to people experiencing critical mental ill-health.

The rollercoaster ride had begun.

We had so many questions, and no one had answers.

The hospital system for any medical condition is a 'mindfield' – yes, my word. I call it this as there is so much information for our brains to take in, unfamiliar words, new meanings to learn and medical language to absorb. Not to mention navigating hospitals, services, and medications, while worrying about an ill loved one, is a mindfield. Different terminologies abound, and with them come new acronyms that need to be explained every time we hear them.

When the tentacles of mental ill-health wrapped around us, we felt helpless. There was no one who spoke any sense to us, it was all medical jargon about the processes of the brain and blah blah blah. Most of it was white noise, and I'm a nurse. The one thing I did hear was that a formal diagnosis of a 'psychiatric condition' could take years. My heart sank. Could we live in the unknown for that long? Could she?

Our girl needed medical assistance and treatment. We needed patience. We needed to focus on the now and work the rest out later, when we had time to breathe.

We all began to learn to live with this new normal. It wasn't easy. There were steps forward and steps back, and days that were just too hard. Through it all, we stayed silent. We closed ranks against the stigma and stereotypes and did our best to protect our daughter and ourselves from assumptions, harmful or not.

My outlet over those years was writing. I filled page after page with raw emotions, hopes and dreams, and shattered realities. I thought I had the draft of an article, but I had way too much information for that. What could I do with it?

Dear Carer,

My first book, *Dear Psychosis,* was born. This was the story I had needed to hear when mental ill-health knocked at our door. A memoir about our family living with and through a major mental health crisis, and learning to live with a chronic illness. Our story reached further than we ever thought. Many people thanked us for breaking the silence that others living and caring for someone with complex mental health conditions could not.

My heart is full of pride in what we have achieved, but I felt it was not quite enough. I had a powerful desire to contribute to the mental health space. I'd come alive speaking to others at libraries, workplaces, with carers, journalists, and podcasters. I would sparkle when I was talking about complex mental health.

My focus shifted from being a caregiver and advocate for my daughter to concentrating on supporting caregivers. I was constantly seeking ways to ease their journey, now or in the future. I decreased my perioperative (operating theatre) job down to one day a week and started working as a carer peer worker – an advocate with lived experience – for committees at a local public hospital.

A teeny-tiny sparkle of an idea gave me my revelation moment about my future direction. Another book that I had needed.

Chapter 2
The seeds of Dear Carer,

The better equipped we are, the more options we will have when a situation arises.

— Sarah

That sparkle of an idea appeared when I started working with carer peer workers and advocating for carers. It helped me see a gap. A gap in mental health services that I and my family had struggled through. Carers often find themselves terrified, faced with a mountain of new information and unthinkable decisions.

What was missing?

A simple guide on what to do when faced with the sudden onset of complex mental health conditions. A resource to share what might happen in the emergency room and during a hospital stay for a loved one. A summary of the roles of the many health professionals who may be involved in recovery. And, perhaps most importantly, a platform for the voices of carers themselves.

Dear Carer,

In the uncharted territory of mental ill-health, we don't know what that next minute, hour, day, or month will look like. This can be unsettling, and learning to go with the flow is easier said than done. The better equipped we are, the more options we will have when a situation arises.

Whether that be medical help and intervention, calling emergency services, having a shower, walking the dog, or visiting the crystal shop. If you've tried it and it works, log it and put it in your toolkit. If it doesn't work, still place the idea in your kit, and save it for later. Being armed with a list of do's and don'ts will help future you, or perhaps a friend, going through something similar.

In the chapters ahead, I will explore a wide range of topics, including grief, sadness, trauma-informed care, wills and power of attorney, together with the hospital admission process from the emergency department to the psychiatric unit and home.

I have interviewed a diverse group of people, many of whom prefer to remain unnamed because of their positions and workplaces, but who were eager to share their knowledge, experience, and expertise.

Additionally, I will provide insights into the roles of police and paramedics, offering practical advice on the do's and don'ts when calling emergency services. We will delve into the realities behind the closed doors of a maximum-security prison and examine the admission process there.

Hearing from a general practitioner, a psychiatrist, and a psychologist adds more to our knowledge bank for the future. We hear from carers around the world, their thoughts, feelings and lived experience, the true experts of their lives and stories.

There's a lot to unpack and talk about, but mostly, I want to put the power back in your hands. I know you may not want to read all the chapters, and that's okay. Skipping pages to get to the relevant stuff is what it's all about.

Every page is bound with love, compassion and strength, for

those who have walked this path and for those who are coming after us. My hope is that *Dear Carer,* adds to your toolkit, expands your knowledge and shows that you are never alone.

Chapter 3
Early Care

Early care can be an overwhelming time for carers; this is not the role or job we thought we'd be living.'

— Sarah

When do you flip the switch or push the button to acknowledge that your loved one needs more care that you alone can give them? When does your care become not enough? When do those flickering thoughts evolve into something concerning? When does that awareness become an 'aha' moment that our loved one needs medical assistance?

When does early care start?

It will be different for us all. Early care starts when you realise or are told – by a friend, health care worker, or perhaps by your loved one – that something is not right

Any thoughts my husband and I had of 'something's not quite

right' were confirmed for us when a stranger called to tell us our daughter was ill. '*With what*?' we asked.

'Some sort of mental health crisis' he said.

When we think back, we could see those tiny tentacles of mental ill-health. The fact is, we didn't act on our concerns. For me, there was guilt that I'd swept those tentacles aside and ignored them. However, 'if only's' are not in our vocabulary anymore. Instead of the shoulda, woulda, coulda's, we deal in the now.

Early care can start as preventative care, if you first see the signs before a crisis arrives. But often those early signs go unnoticed, or are attributed to something else. In that case, early care starts when you, your loved one or someone else presses that 'action stations' button.

Diagnosing complex mental health conditions takes time. It's like completing a jigsaw puzzle. If a doctor or medical team are missing pieces, then a diagnosis will be harder and take longer to discover. We know our medical system is flawed. Our health care workers are stretched beyond capacity, and our hospitals are bursting at the seams with patients requiring assistance, just like our loved ones. Patience is key, but feeling frustrated at delays is valid.

With hindsight, I would have spoken much sooner to a mental health peer worker. Peer workers are trained professionals with lived experience who can support, guide and advocate for others who are going through similar things. Their job titles under the mental health setting are carer peer worker and consumer peer worker. A carer peer worker has lived experience of caring for someone with complex mental health concerns; a consumer peer worker has personal experience of living with complex mental health concerns.

How can we make early care easier?

It can be helpful to establish roles, and what they entail, for family members and others involved in recovery. The earlier you can manage this, the better.

Dear Carer,

My role was that of an inquisitor, the one who questioned everything medically related.

My husband held a support role, ensuring that my stress and guilt didn't consume me. He did all the stuff I couldn't. He kept working, paid the bills, and tried to keep some semblance of normal family life while our girl was in and out of hospital.

Our youngest was thirteen and did what most kids do - went to school, did homework and played outside with friends in the street. That was his role, although a laminated page of emergency and mental health hotline numbers stuck to the fridge was a sign that life had changed for him too.

Our oldest, a down-to-earth guy, was in his final year of medicine. He kept us grounded and ensured that our own mental health was stable. His role was to call us out if we needed a reality check – he asked us how we were going, how we were feeling, and what our stress levels were. And offered gentle reminders to look after *us*, too.

Our daughter played a leading role, doing everything in her power to get better. Emotions during her recovery often ran high; complex mental health symptoms differ greatly, and there was a lot to navigate carefully. During this time, my husband and I became her everything. Her worst enemies, her teachers, and her friends. And as hard as things were at times ... we gave her unconditional love.

My sister was a bit further removed from the day-to-day of recovery. Her role was providing compassion and a non-judgemental space for me to float ideas, talk about my day, be sad and cry if I felt the need.

Our family became a team working in unison. The left hand knew what the right was doing ... well, most of the time.

Who is on your team and what are their roles?

Work out in your family or carer setting what roles you will all play. They can be flexible; nothing needs to be set in stone, and roles can be revisited at any time. What works this month may not work the next. If that happens, change things up, revisit, and then settle down to business.

Consider things that you and others who are helping like doing.

Are you chatty and confident? You might be well placed to ask questions to medical personnel and take notes in appointments

Are you a manager? Organising appointments, managing schedules and paying invoices may be for you.

There are roles for your children, (no matter their age), friends, and others to play. These could include reading a book or playing an instrument with or to their loved one, going for a walk around the block or exercising with them; going with their loved one to art or music therapy, cooking or baking with them.

Holding space and loving them for who they are is perhaps the most precious.

Your team and their roles

The lead: your loved one, who is ill – their role is to focus on getting better

The conductor: the primary carer for your loved one – may be responsible for managing appointments, medications, tracking recovery and reporting back to family and friends on how your loved one is healing.

The main supporter: may continue working outside the home; organises cashflow – money coming in (income, government payments, etc) and money going out (bills, rent/mortgage, etc). Dependable, with inner strength – they quietly get the job done.

Covering all bases: It may be that you're holding all of these titles - doing everything. Please look after yourself, reach out to medical services or mental health organisations.

The best buddy: has a bit of emotional distance; can be a sounding board or someone to vent to. An important role to fill. Steady and reliable.

The ensemble or support crew: these may be your children (no matter the age), a select few family members or friends. Life does and will go on – these are your support crew, that will cheer you on, or be there for you, when you need them most.

It's time to start a spreadsheet

Early care can be an overwhelming time for carers; this is likely not a role we thought we'd be doing. Life truly brings unexpected times, and this is one of them. But there are things we can do to help manage this challenging time, and to help our loved ones self-manage.

I found it helpful to have a 'toolkit' or 'action plan'. I have a notebook and a spreadsheet where everything is in the one place: notes that help our loved one, and us, reminders of what has and hasn't worked in any given situation. Ideas for future care informed by past care, and simple, handy tips and more complex notes that we can have at hand when speaking with medical personnel.

Here's an example

- Diagnosis (if established) eg schizoaffective disorder
- Medical history (eg broken left ankle 2016, appendix removed 2024, admission x 3 for psychosis March 2018 / October 2024 / December 2025
- Medication - drug name, dosage, time administered
- Treating doctors (GP, psychologist etc) eg Dr Smith GP, Dr Beard psychiatrist
- Allergies eg nil known drug allergies, lactose intolerant
- Physical needs (glasses, hearing aids, mobility aids etc)
- Sensitivities or things that cause strong emotional reactions eg does not like loud noises (headphones help), has had a negative experience with needles (injections and insertion of cannulas), heat packs and numbing cream improved the situation thirty minutes prior to canulation

As carers we will have found many tips and tools that help our loved ones and, let's face it, many that haven't. Listing all these things, the positive and the negative, means we don't have to keep them all in our mind. Over time, we will develop a toolkit that we – and others caring for our loved one – can dip into.

For example, there may have been a time when having blood taken didn't go to plan. Document what happened in your spreadsheet with a tip or note to use cream to numb your loved one's skin thirty minutes prior to the procedure. Or to remind your loved one to take their headphones so they can listen to their favourite music as a distraction. Or to ask that the student phlebotomist not to take your loved one's blood.

Chapter 4
What goes in your toolkit?

Turn that computer on and open a spreadsheet or grab a pen and paper to start writing.

Build Your Own Toolkit

Make yourself a list of anything that make life easier for all. Include the elements of your family situation and loved one's traits that might help you help your loved one, and ultimately yourself. Even if something sounds ludicrous, write it down. Include everything – you can slim it down later.

I have included ideas for list items below. Feel free to add, subtract or use something entirely different. The purpose of your toolkit is to make *your* life easier.

Let's start with our emergency medical history – if future-you needs to call emergency services, this can be the start of a checklist that helps first responders understand the situation.

General Information to have ready

- Diagnosis (if known)
- Medical history
- Medication - times and doses
- Allergies
- Treating psychiatrist
- Treating psychologist
- General practitioner
- Sensitivities or things that cause strong emotional reactions
- Guardianship. If you have the document, have it printed and ready to hand to staff. Keep more than one copy.

Do you or your loved one have known emotional reactions to certain circumstances?

Below are some things that commonly cause heightened emotional responses – if you can anticipate and manage these, you can make things that little bit easier for all.

Lack of sleep - Nap during the day (but not too long that night time sleep is affected).

Lack of routine and structure - Ask for collaboration and assistance from your loved one to draw up a schedule that suits you both (and other household members, as needed). But be aware that they may not have the capacity to be involved with decision making.

Is it the end of the world if routine goes out today? No. Sometimes we all need a pyjama day and that's ok.

Overstimulation - (from socialising, gatherings, television, radio, social media)

Noise - Use headphones, noise cancelling if possible, or earplugs or earphones. Establish a quiet space where your loved one can go, perhaps a bean bag or hammock. Preferably not in their bedroom.

Gaming/television/screen irritability - Decrease hours spent on screens. Make sure you discuss your reasons and be prepared for robust discussions, but choose your battles. Establish boundaries (in collaboration with your loved one, if possible). Think of alternatives – books, puzzles, craft, music.

Working out how to manage or avoid strong emotional reactions is difficult. Speak frankly with your loved one about what they find difficult, and to the medical team while your loved one is still in hospital (if they have been admitted). Being prepared and asking questions adds to your toolkit for later. Remember, whatever questions you have for your mental health team, it will not be the first time they have heard them. Use their wealth of knowledge to help *you*. Speak with other carers and ask them to share their experiences, positive *and* negative.

Add these and any other tips or ideas you can think of to your toolkit.

Some more important information for your toolkit

Personal, family, and cultural factors

- Is your loved one part of the LGBTQIA+ community, or are they neurodiverse? What do health professionals need to know to make treatment or an admission easier?
- Are you from a culturally and linguistically diverse (CALD) background?
- Is there a language barrier? Is an interpreter required? Try to ensure that the department or office you are going to is aware that an interpreter is required when the appointment is made.
- If your loved one can speak and understand English, is this the time that others need a reminder to speak clearly?
- Is your loved one Aboriginal or Torres Strait Islander? What elements of cultural identity need to be noted and respected? (Eg women's/men's business)
- Do you or your loved one require culturally sensitive support? The national Aboriginal Community Controlled Health Organisation (NACCHO) is the national peak body that represents Aboriginal community-controlled health organisations (ACCHO) across Australia. Contact your local organisation or ask your social worker to put you in touch with the best service for your circumstances.

Medication

Early care might be when your loved one first starts taking medication for their mental health. There is much to unpack regarding medications, whether that be stigma, compliance or non-compliance, or our loved ones not having insight as to why they should take them. Having options for resolutions on hand is a positive.

Medications not taken on time or missed

Brain fog is often reported by people experiencing mental ill-health. If remembering to take medications is a challenge in your household, you could try:

- Purchasing medication pill boxes or containers.
- Setting alarms.
- Writing when to take it (day / a.m. / p.m) on the packet with a permanent marker.
- Asking your pharmacist to make up blister packs.

Medication non-compliance

This is a hard one, and finding a solution can be difficult. If your loved one is able to discuss not taking medication, try to find out why they might be avoiding it. Some common reasons are:

- Weight gain
- Feeling like a zombie – sleeping all hours and waking up foggy.
- The feelings or thoughts they have when taking medication.
- Your loved one doesn't need it.
- Side effects – note these down and present them to your medical team. Do not treat any of these lightly as some can be debilitating.

Keeping your medical team informed of any non-compliance is very important. Medications that work for me or my loved one might not have the same interaction with you or your loved one, so don't compare with others. Time and patience are needed as some medications take a few weeks to begin working within our bodies.

Thinking outside the box can and does bring solutions.

- Can this medication be given intramuscularly instead of orally?
- Can this medication be given in a syrup form instead of a tablet?
- Can the tablets be crushed or the capsule be opened and taken in the powder form?

Discuss all these options with your medical team or psychiatrist. Don't assume anything – different medications are absorbed and processed differently by our bodies. The powder may need that capsule around it; a tablet may need to be taken in whole form and not crushed.

Let's talk about drug and alcohol abuse

There is no doubt that prevention, early intervention, and specialised care are needed with drug and alcohol abuse. Substance abuse and addiction are complex issues, but note that at least fifty five per cent of people experiencing an alcohol and other drug disorder have a co-occurring mental health condition.[1]

If you are concerned about substance use, seek advice from specialised mental health drug and alcohol units across Australia. Advise them that there is an existing mental health concern *and* substance use. Ensure that any treating mental health team are aware, so that additional support can be given to avoid, reduce or modify the substance or substances used.

The term 'no wrong door' is used for an approach that ensures that one specialist can provide treatment that is specific to their patient. Your loved one should have their mental health care *and* drug and alcohol use treated by the same medical team.

1. https://adf.org.au/resources/health-professionals/aod-mental-health/

Chapter 5
Emergency Service Care

> It's important to share everything you know about the incident with the operator on the phone prior to the arrival of emergency services.
>
> — Sarah

We call emergency services because a major incident has occurred. Stress, anxiety, and concern levels are high for all, carers, the loved one we're worried about, bystanders, and whoever is making the call.

What to share with emergency services

It's important to share everything you know about the incident with the phone operator prior to the arrival of emergency services; the dispatcher relays that information to the team coming to you.

Safety is always a priority. If possible, callers or carers should identify and advise on risks, such as aggressive behaviour or access to, or use of, a weapon that may cause harm to emergency services or others.

Provide background information including diagnosis, medication, strong emotional reactions, history with police and/or hospital, and any propensity to violence. If you don't have any knowledge, say so.

Advise if there are barriers to communication with the patient, including auditory hallucinations, language barriers, disabilities, or others.

Other important things to tell the emergency operator include:

- Overdose or ingestion of a substance. Provide any information you have about what has been ingested. This information is extremely helpful to emergency services.
- If the patient has harmed themself, you or somebody else (and the condition of the person harmed).
- If there has been suicidal ideation or a suicide attempt.
- If the patient has threatened you or someone else.
- A list of the patient's medications, and whether these have been taken as prescribed.
- Allergies.
- Anything else that is causing you concern.

Calling emergency services

Remain calm. I know it's easy to say and hard to do. Take a steadying breath and remind yourself that you are advocating for the safety of your loved one.

Tell the operator what service you require: Fire. Police. Ambulance. You may require one or all three, and that is okay. Depending on the situation, the operator may notify multiple services.

Provide current incident information. If you have the

address, give it to them. They will ask for the nearest road, intersection or cross street, building, or any landmark that is significant, and/or the town, suburb, and state.
Stay calm. Panic induces panic. Take another deep breath and blow it out slowly.
The operator may ask:

- your name and contact details.
- what made you call emergency services (eg, talk of suicide or harm to you or your loved one themself).
- what injuries have been sustained, if any.
- if you, your loved one, or someone else is an imminent threat or at risk (e.g. they have a weapon).

Stay on the line. Remain calm and focused. Assistance is on the way.

The conversation may go something like this

000 operator: What's your emergency? Fire, ambulance, police?

Caller: We need an ambulance.

000 operator: Transferring.

Ambulance operator: State your town and your location.

Caller: ACT, Canberra, Syd.

Ambulance operator: What's the address please.

Caller: We are at 2 Smith Street in a suburb called Syd in Canberra, ACT.

Ambulance operator: What's the nearest intersection or cross street there?

Caller: It has a McDonalds on the corner; I don't recall the name of the street.

Ambulance operator: I'm sending someone now. Stay on the line.

Ambulance operator: Can you tell me what's happened?

Caller: My son is not well. He is seeing things that aren't there and I don't understand what he's talking about. He says that his head hurts, and he's pulling at his hair and slapping his face.

The operator may ask you to stay on the line until emergency services arrive or give you instructions to meet the emergency services that have been dispatched.

When paramedics arrive

If your loved one is a danger to others, paramedics must wait until the police arrive. Their priority is safety; this action ensures it. If paramedics are standing back, it is not because they do not want to treat your loved one. It is because it is unsafe for them to do so. When paramedics can treat your loved one, stand back and allow them to do so.

They will ask the patient questions. Remember, these are for the *patient* to answer, *not you*. Paramedics will ask what's happening and why they have been called. They will ask about their mental health, assess their vital signs, and treat any wounds or injuries.

Paramedics may ask you or others at the scene for information if the patient is unable or unwilling to talk. When asked for more information, be clear and concise.

Your loved one may refuse care. This may be distressing and confusing for you. They also may lack awareness and insight into what is happening. If this happens, further discussions will take place with emergency workers regarding the risk your loved one poses to themselves or others. This may lead to your loved one being involuntarily admitted to hospital, for the safety of themself and/or others.

Sometimes we need to stand back and let emergency services do their thing. This is one of those times. As much as it may frustrate or upset you, stand back. They know you are there, and if they need to ask further questions of you, they will.

When police arrive

The first officers to arrive will need to evaluate the situation. Remember, police officers receive training to handle individuals with complex mental health concerns, but they lack clinical training. They are not health workers, but they are here to assist your loved one and you. This can be a confronting and upsetting time. The more information you can give police, the more knowledge they will have on how to best help your loved one.

When they arrive, stand back and allow the police to focus on doing their job; they will ask you for any pertinent information when they are ready. If you are the enduring guardian and have documentation stating this, have it with you so that emergency services can note it. If your loved one is going to the hospital, take the documentation with you. While emergency services are assisting your loved one, go and pack any items that they may need for a hospital stay.

Dear Carer,

Let's add a selection of items for a hospital toolkit:

- Medication.
- Glasses.
- Hearing aid.
- Sanitary items.
- Personal care items, toothpaste, toothbrush, hairbrush, etc.
- Enduring guardianship.
- Clothing without cords.
- Shoes without shoelaces.
- Items that help with self-soothing.
- Phones and chargers are generally not permitted on the ward - cords can be a safety risk, as they could harm themselves or others.

Chapter 6
Stories and lives of our emergency workers

Over the next few pages, you will hear the voices of a paramedic and a police negotiator who have attended patients with complex mental health conditions. You may have had experiences that gave you a negative perception of these service providers; I'm hoping to share that, behind the uniforms, police and paramedics are people, like us.

Out of respect, the identity of these emergency workers will remain private. Each person I spoke to has been given a pseudonym. Each person I spoke to has opened my eyes and my heart.

Chapter 7
Cassi's story: through a paramedic's eyes

If safe to do so, a straightforward way to help assist paramedics de-escalate a situation is to notify the patient that we have been called prior to our arrival.

— Cassi

I had the honour of talking with Cassi, a paramedic who works in one of the busiest regions of New South Wales. She shared what a regular day looks like, when additional support for paramedics is required, and what we – as carers – can do to help them.

Cassi, what does a day in the life of a paramedic look like?

I became a paramedic through the graduate pathway. This involved completing a bachelor's degree, which consisted of three years at university, followed by a year of probational on-road training.

As a paramedic, I work a rotating shift pattern of four days on (including two days, two nights), and five days off. We work with the same partner for a nine-week block, and the shifts are 12 hours long. Each day is different, and we can cover a wide geographical area, as we can be dispatched anywhere depending on operational demand. Our day looks like this:

- Each shift starts out of our home station.
- We sign on to an ambulance and complete all mandatory checks of drugs and equipment.
- Once we are operationally ready, dispatch allocates jobs to attend. Allocation involves a multitude of factors, including clinical priority of the job, clinical skill level, and distance to the job.
- Each call out consists of responding to the location, patient assessment and management, transportation, and transfer of care.
- Once the job is completed, we will be dispatched to our next job.

What training in psychiatric health do you receive?

What we receive is minimal, and most of our training occurs on the job. I recall one unit of my university degree focusing on mental health training. This was followed by brief training throughout my internship regarding specific mental health legislation, assessment, and management. I learnt through on-the-job exposure and by observing how my mentors interacted with patients suffering an acute psychiatric health crisis.

This is an area that needs more attention and training, considering the current prevalence of cases, and it is pleasing to know that there have been inroads in increasing the psychiatric health education of our paramedics that are currently in training.

Cassi, what can we, the carer or caller, do to de-escalate a situation when paramedics arrive?

If safe to do so, a straightforward way to help assist paramedics de-escalate a situation is to notify the patient that we have been called prior to our arrival.

When we arrive, if possible, it is useful for us to have a brief private conversation to understand the caller's concerns, the patient's condition, and their behaviour leading up to the call.

It can also be helpful to know if the patient has any strong emotional reactions, and strategies to de-escalate their behaviour.

I don't know exactly how many calls we receive a day for mental health. However, on average, I would attend at least one call per shift for a patient suffering an acute mental health crisis.

When and why would you request police backup?

Police assistance is requested on any job where we have concerns for safety, including to the patient, public, and ourselves.

In some cases, we may request police attendance based on the notes we receive regarding the case. Information provided by the caller may identify concerning reports, for example, weapons involved. In these cases, we will request police attendance and wait until their arrival. After the police arrive, we will proceed with the job once they have made the scene safe.

In other cases, where we have already contacted the patient, we may request police assistance if the patient or scene escalates. If a patient becomes threatening, violent, or aggressive, or if a patient who has been placed under the mental health act needs transport and refuses to cooperate with paramedics, we may request police assistance.

We commonly attend jobs that end up being different from what we are initially called to. In the instance where it becomes a mental health job, we perform a brief risk assessment to ensure our safety. The majority of the time, the scene is deemed safe, and we are able to proceed with our mental health assessment and management. In the case of it being deemed unsafe, we retreat to our ambulance and a safe location until police can attend the job.

In some states of Australia, there are mental health nurses and clinicians that assist paramedics and police on a mental health call out. Does this happen where you are?

Currently in my place of employment this is not occurring. However, there is a 'PACER' team that consists of the Police, Ambulance and a Clinician who are part of an Early Response program. This includes a mental health clinician being paired with an emergency worker to provide community assessment and support to patients suffering from mental ill-health.

Your profession provides unique insights most of us do not see. How do you cope?

The biggest support I have found whilst working as a paramedic is having a dedicated support network. I wouldn't be able to continue this line of work without the immense support of my partner, friends, and family. I also ensure that I maintain a healthy work and life balance. When I am on days off, I fill my cup with things that make me happy, quality time with loved ones, reading, exercising and walking my dog. I also access a private psychologist to help regulate my own work-life stresses.

Does work provide you with access to counselling or psychologists?

We do have access to a psychologist who is employed by the service, to reach out to if required. Accessing a psychologist is a straightforward process, and we are normally able to arrange an appointment quickly. I believe the mental wellbeing of paramedics is an area that requires improvement. In my personal experience, it is common to work a twelve hour-plus shift with no break, and when combining this with attending difficult jobs, having little family time between shifts, being unable to access regular exercise whilst on shift, and having limited leave to reset, my cup can empty quickly.

Cassi, what would you tell your younger self?

I would tell younger me to always be kind to myself and to prioritise my physical and mental health. And to always surround myself with happiness and love.

Chapter 8
Jane's story: looking beyond the uniform of our police force

> 'I will speak to someone face to face where they are at, on a roof, in a house, on a bridge.'
>
> —Jane

I spoke with Jane, a current member of the police force, whose role is a police negotiator. I'm not sure what I was expecting, but what I gained was knowledge and insight into a profession that needs to dot every 'i' and cross every 't'. What I heard was compassion, strength, patience, and resilience.

Jane, what does the role of police negotiator involve?

As a police negotiator, I have a unique perspective. I engage with people in absolute crisis, often for hours and hours on end.

I see their illness move in and out, duck and weave.
I see and hear when voices take over and when they quieten.

I see and hear the decision-making process when one is contemplating taking their life.

First responders have a role in immediate safety for all. They are there to quickly resolve, to either have the person taken to hospital or left to their own devices depending on circumstances. They don't have the time to find out the patient's why or how, and more and more they are forced to speed things up and get to the outcome.

As a negotiator, I have all the time in the world. I am there to engage with our patient. That is my focus. I will speak to someone face to face where they are at – on a roof, in a house, on a bridge – and try to hear their why or how. I have developed a deep understanding of the black hole they have found themselves in to get to that point.

What have you learnt as a negotiator?

As a negotiator, I have received extensive training in developing rapport and effective communication. I find in my conversations with these people that they crave being heard; they want to feel seen and believed. They want validation of their decision to take themselves off medication. I listen, but I don't necessarily tell them I think they are doing the right thing. But I make sure they know I understand their reasons.

Once I have spent time getting to know the how and why, I try to bring some hope and practical options to the table. I talk through how a hospital admission may work, some success stories with alternative medication plans, and what moving through this period might look like.

I always try to find something that makes them light up inside. A loved one, a pet, an achievement. Something that still brings joy. And I bring them back to that thought a few times when I feel they might be slipping away.

I never lie. I never promise something I can't deliver or that won't happen. They teach us that from day one. We cannot expect to be believed if we have lied, and if that person is in crisis again, they won't forget that lie.

I often distance myself from armed or uniformed police at the scene, as they can feel scary. I identify myself as a police officer, but one who's there just to talk. I tell them I won't force them into any decision, but I can help them talk through things. I promise them I won't try to grab them, but I will encourage them to move a little closer to me and safety. I only ever bring them down on their terms and their timeframe.

If it takes all day and all night, I'm there with them.

There are times when no amount of talking will work. They cannot hear or comprehend. When the other sounds are louder, and I can't get a peek into the window of their eyes, I will talk and talk to myself for hours in the hope of seeing a glimmer of response. But eventually someone might make the decision to try to find another solution, which may mean a tactically planned grab.

I have not yet (touch wood) lost someone in my negotiations. All have found a way to come down from a ledge, drop a weapon, put down something dangerous and walk calmly towards me. I give them a hug, tell them I'm proud of them – because I am! It's not easy to back down when you go so far.

I make notes of our conversations, recording details of what was said. But our actual conversations are never recorded. I want there to be something useful available that someone else might use should they find themselves with that person and I can't be there.

Police too often treat psychiatric patients like criminals. I've seen it, and I have seen how it can happen. Some patients are actual criminals, some do criminal stuff, and yes, some are dangerous. Some are so drug affected, it's hard to know. But who fits in which category can be challenging to determine in the space of a second when a reaction or decision is needed.

Most people I speak to are unheard, misunderstood, fighting something invisible that's difficult for us to grasp. I wish there were a lot more mental health training for police. It would mean fewer people hurt, more dignity and respect, and a greater understanding of our fellow human beings.

Jane, what education do you receive about complex mental health conditions in the police force?

Our yearly mental health and psychiatric training is face-to-face, via PowerPoint, for about two hours. Whilst it's an interesting session, it shows a lot of *You Can't Ask That* footage. There is no practical component or even much chance for discussion. The takeaway message is along the lines of, 'there are many psychiatric illnesses, but you will unlikely be able to work out which one you're seeing; the symptoms and behaviours all overlap, and mental health patients are unpredictable.'

I completed a four day course many years ago but have likely not retained all the information. The police negotiators course focuses heavily on psychiatric health. There are days and days of lectures and presentations, which are highly informative. More training needs to be given from the perspective of patients with psychiatric concerns. How they see, feel, perceive the police and their surroundings.

Sounds like you could use more training

There is definitely not enough training. Regional police have limited resources, so need even more training. There are multiple call outs per day every day for mental health, and it's increasing. If they could implement it, a mental-health first-aid course would be a powerful addition.

Jane, when someone has called emergency services, what should they do when you arrive?

Often if police are called, the person cannot manage or control the patient, so it's sometimes better they step out of sight. The radio operator will provide warnings from the caller to police, but more can be achieved if the carer or person who called can speak to a second police officer while another officer engages with the patient. When you call the police for mental health concerns, an ambulance is put on the job and asked to attend, as it's recommended they transport all patients – not the police.

Last question but an important one. Who looks after you?

We have access to psychologists. But this is rarely used by most. Phone consults are easy, but for a face-to-face there is a longer wait time.

I think most serving police officers are coping okay, but more ease of access to an in-person mental health clinician would be useful. We have one at the station I'm currently at, who comes around one day a week. Police are notoriously bad at asking for help for themselves, so mandatory check-ins would be great for all police, not just specific duty types, as is the case.

With so much going on in a day's work, I need to compartmentalise. I also meditate and exercise. I also need to be resilient, as each day at work can bring different challenges. I definitely need family time, friends, scrolling, wine and, without a doubt, humour.

Chapter 9
The Telephone Game

As children, we used to play a game called *telephone*. There'd be ten of us in a line. The first person whispered a phrase into the next person's ear – something like 'the cat sat on the mat and ate porridge with her tiny human.' The second person would whisper what they heard into the next person's ear, and so on down the line. By the time the phrase was whispered to the last person, it would have become something like, 'a car went down the street in an ice cream.' This makes no sense!

You may need to repeat information to many different health care workers, from emergency workers to the medical staff at the hospital. No matter how many times you or your loved one repeats their medical history to a doctor, nurse, social worker or whoever, it should come *directly* from your mouth to their ears without anyone in between to interpret it differently. I know the repetition is beyond frustrating, but no matter how many times you share your loved one's signs, symptoms and medical history, remember this. *Your words to their ears*. There can be no miscommunication.

Chapter 10
Emergency Room Care to Recovery care

'Remember, your loved one has the right to not give consent for you to know their medical information. If this happens, let the doctor or nurse know that, after their consultation, you have more information to share'.

— Sarah

From the emergency department to the psychiatric unit

Regardless of why we go to the hospital emergency room, our first question is, how long before we will be seen or admitted? This is talked about no matter what state or country we live in. We need an abundance of patience not to feel frustrated at the length of time we sit and wait, and this can be even harder if we are waiting with a loved one experiencing psychosis, suicidal thoughts, or any other mental health concerns.

Hospital staff are often overworked, some working overtime and others handling double the workload because of illness, not enough staff to cover the shift, or annual leave. These are not excuses for long wait times. Our governments need to do better with resourcing emergency departments. But no matter how busy they are, the emergency staff are as desperate as the patients they see to make a positive change for all.

Knowing this doesn't relieve our anxiety, concern and frustration, especially when sitting next to a loved one who has the tentacles of mental ill-health wrapped tightly around them. But it can help us remember that emergency room staff are people too. I can only say, even if you have been waiting for hours, you are in the best place possible for your loved one at this time. I know these might seem like empty words, but in the absence of specialised complex mental health facilities, the emergency department is the safest place to be.

What to bring to the emergency room for your loved one:

- Medications.
- Headphones or earbuds to lessen the noise in the department.
- Guardianship documentation.
- Self-soothing items such as fidgets.
- Eye mask.
- Change of clothes.
- Toiletries.
- Snacks and water. Be mindful, as fasting may be required for tests or surgery.

Items for the carer:

- Phone charger.
- Documentation of events as you know them.
- Book, knitting, crochet, drawing.
- Headphones, earbuds for podcast, audiobook or music.

- Patience, pack that too.

Build your own toolkit for hospital - some examples

- Medication - drug name / dosage / administration times.
- Glasses - needs glasses at all times.
- Hearing aid - hearing aids needed both ears.
- Sanitary items - will not use tampons / pads only.
- Enduring guardianship - yes – in email /photocopy available.
- Clothing without cords, shoes without shoelaces, slippers/Ugg boots.
- Items that help with self-soothing.

Emergency room care

Whether you, someone else, police or paramedics have taken your loved one to hospital, you may not know exactly what will happen next. You are in a safe place. If you look around, you'll see everyone is as desperate, tired, worried and frustrated as each other. We need patience with a dash of hope.

When our loved one is finally seen by the medical team, we can feel unheard and unseen, especially if our loved one has not given their consent for us to receive information about their care and treatment. This does not mean that the medical staff cannot hear the information that we have to share.

As a carer, advocacy is at the heart of what we do. What if we are not with our loved one when they are admitted to hospital? You are well within your rights to contact the hospital and share any information. Vital pieces of the puzzle may be missed. Not due to negligence or incompetence by medical staff, but through lack of information. If they are psychotic, how much insight and capacity does your loved one have to be able to share their medical history, or to articulate what has happened in the lead up to the hospital admission? Sometimes medical staff don't have all the puzzle pieces and must do their best with an incomplete picture.

Below is an example of *why* carers, family or others need to be a part of a solution; we can hold important pieces of the puzzle.

> Nurse 1: Hey, Joe Smith in bed 7 is refusing his medication.

> Nurse 2: He refused this morning as well. It wasn't until I showed him the labels on his tablets that he accepted them. He took them after that, but he's just not listening to anything I say.

> Nurse 1: I'll go do the same thing and see if it makes a difference ... actually, I just thought of something. Is he deaf? You said he didn't listen to you, just wondering as he didn't respond to me either.

In fact, Joe Smith is deaf and cannot lip read. His hearing aids were forgotten after he ripped them out of his ears at home during a psychotic episode. This is a crucial piece of the puzzle. Joe is too unwell to explain, and his carers or those that know him are unaware that the hearing aids are missing. This leads the nurses to assume that Joe is refusing treatment and medications, when in fact this is not the case.

When we finally get past those magical emergency department doors and our loved one is settled into a chair or a bed, the actual relief for us as carers is real. But then we have to wait for the psychiatric consult. The length of time we wait depends on the time of day or night we're there. If it's after hours or on a weekend, get yourself settled – it could be a while.

Your loved one could be seen by, in no particular order, an emergency nurse, an emergency doctor, a mental health nurse, an intern, psychiatric registrar[1] or psychiatrist. In my experience, we never saw the consultant psychiatrist in the emergency department. If you would like to speak with the attending psychiatrist, put in a request with the nursing staff and the psychiatric registrar. They may be able to inform you what time of day they come to do ward rounds.

Each of these medical professionals will come and speak to your loved one, take their medical history, and order any medical tests that they deem necessary.

This is the moment you remember the telephone story from earlier

Remember, all the pieces of the puzzle need to be shared. Your words should go straight to the health care workers' ears. This is NOT the time to leave something out because it was embarrassing, dangerous, frightening, or simply ... odd.

If your loved one has talked about suicide, share those words.
If your loved one has harmed themselves or talked about self-harm, say those words.
Say the words that frighten you.
Say the words.

Remember, your loved one has the right to not give consent for

1. A registrar is a doctor who is training in a specialised medical field, in this case psychiatry. A resident doctor is someone who has finished their basic training and is continuing their medical education. Intern doctors are in their first year of supervised training after finishing their medical degree.

you to know their medical information. If this happens, let the doctor or nurse know that, after their consultation, you have more information to share. I have found that the team will listen and document but will give nothing in return other than a nod and a thank you. Patients have a right to privacy, and staff have a responsibility to uphold that. And as hard as it may be in the stress of the moment, we need to accept it.

> *Now that your loved one has been admitted to the unit, the mental health team will work towards the goal of recovery. We attempt to implement the least restrictive model of care and, if possible, involve the patient in planning their care in a way that is beneficial to them.*
>
> *Our primary goal is to support the patient at that moment, determining all available options.*
>
> — Trish (mental health nurse)

Breathe

It's here that as a carer your mind may be spinning. The white walls and sterile environment can bring up lots of difficult emotions. But what is the alternative? Our loved one is safe. We are safe. It's time to breathe.

Awareness

When you or others arrive in any psychiatric unit, all visitors will be asked to remove items that may cause a risk to patients, staff or visitors. This might include shoelaces, belts, ties, necklaces, plastic bags, mobile phones, handbags or anything else the unit staff deem necessary. Items will be placed in a locker while you visit. This is for the safety of everyone on the ward.

Guilt

When you walk through the doors of a psychiatric ward, remember: this is not your fault. This is not your loved one's fault. Complex mental health conditions are like any other serious illness. They did not ask for this and, most assuredly, neither did you.

Do me a favour when you leave the ward and walk outside into the open air. No matter the weather, touch the wall, a door, a plant or anything solid. Take a deep breath and try to shrug a little of the guilt and sadness away. Remember, they are safe.

Grief

We do not need someone to die to grieve. We do not need anyone's permission to feel grief. Grieving a person who is ill is natural. It can feel like your loved one has 'disappeared'. There are groups that can help.

Griefline (1300 845 745) is free and funded by the Australian government. It has resources for you and anyone in need. It has forums, education and a helpline. A link is in the 'Links to Resources' section at the end of *Dear Carer*.

Chapter 11
Trish's story: mental health nurse

Once an admission is determined, the emergency room medical team will complete necessary medical tests. These are to rule anything out, or to aid in the treatment that is received.

— Trish

Many years ago, when I did my nursing training, we had a single, solitary 2 hour lecture on complex mental health conditions. I'm glad to say that this has changed. Today, there is more focus on lived experience from a consumer and carer perspective, nursing placements in mental health units, and ongoing mental health education.

Working in the mental health field presents many challenges and we often overlook the remarkable people who care for our loved ones during a hospital admission. I was fortunate to meet and chat with Trish, a mental health nurse who is a clinical nurse consultant (their name badges include the initials CNC) in a public hospital. She shared her insights into what we, as carers, should know during the admission process of a loved one.

Trish, what does a typical workday look like for you?

Most shifts involve a high emotional input, and because of this, I try to erase the previous day's events from my mind. I call it a coping strategy, as vicarious trauma can and does affect clinicians' own mental health. If not addressed, this can lead to burnout.

What qualifications do you hold?

I have a master's degree in addition to my nursing degree. I am required to do mandatory medical training every year. We also receive additional mental health training and supervision at work.

Can you guide us through the admission process?

When someone arrives in the emergency department with psychiatric concerns, the mental health team will be notified and the treating team will discuss guardianship. If the patient has a guardian, then it is good to tell the team now and give them the appropriate documentation. If documentation is unavailable or guardianship is unknown, this is the time to ensure the medical and mental health team are made aware.

A mental health clinical nurse consultant or psychiatric registrar will see your loved one. Occasionally, if within day shift, a psychiatric consultant will review your loved one. Once an admission is determined, the emergency room medical team will complete necessary medical tests. These are to rule anything out, or to aid in the treatment that is received and can include bloodwork, a Covid-19 test, and CT brain scan. Doctors use CT brain scans in mental health admissions to diagnose any brain abnormalities that may cause psychiatric symptoms.

If all is going well, the patient is then cleared to be transferred to a psychiatric unit. Psychiatric emergency care (PECC) and psychiatric units have the same admission process. Admitting a patient can be a confusing time for carers and consumers, so I recommend carers support their loved ones, but also allow treating teams to facilitate a smooth admission. This is often a stressful time for patients, and seeing a family member upset or resistant to an admission can make the experience more traumatising for the patient.

Sadly, a family member once assaulted me while their loved one was being admitted. This elevated the patient's distress and required security and sedation, which we always try to avoid. I sustained an injury. It is important to remember we are here to help your loved one, and you as well.

It is important to note that patients are not left with medications. These will be locked up and administered by nursing staff at the appropriate time. The ward also prohibits sharps to ensure the safety of patients, staff, and visitors, these may include items such as nail clippers and nail scissors.

When is the best time to ask questions about what the course of action is, now that out loved one is in hospital?

Questions can be asked at any time, and while the patient is in the emergency department is a great place to start. If your loved one is admitted to the psychiatric unit, the ward staff can provide more comprehensive answers, so you should ask questions or anything needing clarification there.

I've always wondered, why are visiting hours so specific in a psychiatric unit?

There are a few reasons. One is so patients can focus on their treatment. The ward has a routine with ward rounds, family meetings, meals, and medication times. From a nursing perspective, having visitors on a ward can be wonderful for the patient, and also help staff gain an understanding of relationship dynamics. But we need to take into consideration safety and risks for patients, visitors, and staff. We are also mindful of patient confidentiality.

Trish, knowing what you know now, what advice would you give your younger self?

Buckle up, you're in for a ride! Psychiatric nursing is not for the faint-hearted.

Chapter 12
Medical Care

If it helps, write down your concerns prior to the consult, just so you don't forget things.

— Dr Cal

It can be hard to distinguish what roles medical personnel play. Business suits, white coats, green scrubs, blue scrubs, colourful scrubs, everyday clothing – it gets confusing! Everyone you speak with in a hospital setting should wear a name badge that identifies who they are ... but many don't, and it can be tricky to catch someone's name and role when they're in small text hanging from a lanyard. You have every right to ask for clarification if a staff member doesn't introduce themselves. I have found that it works to stop them, interrupting if necessary, to introduce myself, and then ask them who they are and what their role is. It's not rude, and it is your right.

In addition to medical care, there are many 'alternative treatments' that, as a carer, you may wish to seek out to assist with your loved one's ongoing care. These may include a range of options, from herbal medicine to acupuncture, and many others in between. If you do seek alternative treatments, it is important to mention this to your loved one's treating doctor and medical team to minimise or prevent any adverse reactions.

Seek second opinions and look for testimonials regarding all care, whether medical or alternative therapies. There are people operating under the mental health and medical banner that have no qualifications or right to do so. As carers we need to protect ourselves and our loved ones from those engaging in unqualified practices.

Questions for new providers

- Are your premises accessible?
- Do you provide translation services?
- Do you regularly provide care for people with complex/intersecting diagnoses?
- What are your billing arrangements?
- Will Medicare cover costs?
- What mental health qualifications do you have?
- Do you specialise in a specific illness such as bipolar?
- Can you suggest someone who specialises in schizoaffective disorder?
- Do you have computer / internet capabilities for appointments?
- What is parking like and is it paid parking?
- Are your offices accessible by public transport?
- If you are ill or away, who will care for our loved one?

Dear Carer,

What to do if you have serious concerns regarding the health, care and treatment of someone in hospital

Your treating hospital will have a procedure in place for when there are concerns about a patient's treatment – particularly if their condition is getting worse. In New South Wales, the phrase used is 'Raise It' and the escalation process usually goes:

- Talk to a doctor or nurse regarding your concerns.
- If you are still concerned, ask the nurse in charge for a clinical review.
- If you are still concerned, call the appropriate phone number, it should be clearly displayed in the hospital, if not ask medical personnel.

Many hospitals have a term or phrase that can be used to raise concerns immediately. These can be raised by your loved one or you, the carer. This term or phrase may be different around hospitals in Australia and the world.

Terms used in public hospitals in Australia

New South Wales – 'Raise It'.
Queensland – 'Ryan's Rule'.
Australian Capital Territory – CARE.
Western Australia – Recognising & Responding to Acute Deterioration.
Victoria – 'Hear Me'.
South Australia – You're worried, we're listening.
Northern Territory – Speak to a Consumer Engagement or Patient Liaison.
Tasmania – Speak to a Consumer Engagement or Patient Liaison.

Chapter 13
General practitioner

General practitioners (GP), or local doctors, are who we go to for a broad spectrum of ailments.

They are usually our first port of call when we have a medical problem. If the issue is beyond their scope of practice, they will refer us to a specialist or the most appropriate person or place. Our GP might be the first person we raise mental health concerns with; it may be the first time we have spoken those words aloud.

When I was in Istanbul finding our daughter and bringing her home for medical care, the first thing I asked my husband to do was to call our local doctor. It was important that they be aware of what was coming their way. My husband booked a long appointment for us and gave them the facts. When we arrived at the doctor's rooms, our GP was forearmed with the appropriate knowledge. They were able to direct us to the most appropriate place for immediate treatment – for us, that was the emergency department of our local hospital.

Chapter 14
Dr Cal's story: mental health in general practice

Many carers of people with mental illnesses will know that patients don't always have insight into their condition.

— Dr Cal

I chatted with Dr Cal, a GP with over forty years of clinical experience. They have a passion for mental health and complex mental health conditions.

Dr Cal, what happens when someone presents to you to talk about mental health?

Patients with concerns about the way they are feeling, reacting and even just managing will often present looking for a reason (usually physical) to explain their concerns. This is perfectly reasonable and should be encouraged. If someone you care about appears to be struggling, it is often a less confronting option to suggest they don't appear quite themselves and maybe they should get checked out medically.

It is my experience that people are always more willing to accept a physical diagnosis than a psychological one.

If a patient books an appointment for mental health and a mental health plan is required, what's the course of action?

If a patient comes to discuss a mental health plan, they are already well on the road to recovery. The patient already recognises they have a problem and has accepted they need help. These are two major hurdles already overcome. Help and healing can be accessed, but of course, it isn't always that straightforward.

Sometimes the concerns will all be physical and the fact they are all a manifestation of a psychological illness will have to be teased out, usually over a series of visits. This can get really tricky, but hopefully the picture will become clearer with time and perseverance. If a patient says, 'I'm concerned I might have depression' or 'I feel anxious all the time' – that's a starting point.

The doctor will first take a full history and examination – looking for any conditions that could be causing the symptoms, such as anaemia, thyroid disease, and heart arrhythmias. There's no definitive blood test for anxiety or depression (or bipolar, obsessive-compulsive disorder and others); it is a clinical diagnosis, and you have to be sure other possible diagnoses have been excluded. Even if you are sure the issue is not physical but psychological, you also need to check for other factors, such as psychosis or mania or substance abuse, which would need more specialist care.

At the other end of the scale, anxiety and depression can be physiological, the body functioning in a normal and healthy way, rather than pathological, which involves abnormalities and deviations within the body. If a patient is grieving or stressed by too much work, then feeling depressed or anxious would be a normal reaction under such circumstances. At this point, the doctor is determining if the patient is mentally unwell and, if so, how severe is this mental illness.

It's not always easy and we certainly don't always get it right, but that is what we should do.

Dr Cal, how can we make these consultations easier?

Very reasonable question, because it is often difficult for a person who is in the throes of mental illness to actually articulate what the issues are and how they feel.

It helps if you have an established relationship with your doctor, because hopefully they will be able to recognise changes in behaviour, thinking, mood, etc. It always helps if you start with the symptoms that concern you the most. If you've always been a worrier, but now you can't leave home without checking the door is locked twenty times and you are now always late, start with that. If it helps, write down your concerns prior to the consult, just so you don't forget things.

Many carers of people with mental illnesses will know that patients don't always have insight into their condition. Over many years in general practice, I have been contacted by relatives and carers who have expressed concerns that their loved one is mentally unwell (more commonly with dementia, admittedly, but also with anxiety, anorexia, depression, mania – even a gambling addiction, which I hadn't suspected at all). Of course, I'm not allowed to discuss a patient's condition without the patient's permission, but I'm allowed to listen and have always appreciated the heads up.

Ultimately getting the diagnosis is the key. Once this is established, the next major step is knowledge. Patients don't always readily accept they have a mental illness, but it really needs to be seen in the same category as diabetes or asthma. It has an underlying cause, manifestations, presentations, a natural history, exacerbating factors and, most importantly, a range of treatment options. It is usually at this point a mental health care plan will be offered.

Creating a mental health care plan takes a minimum of twenty minutes, but probably closer to forty minutes, and is usually done at a dedicated consultation. The actual plan is documentation of the patient's diagnosis, where they are now, what treatment and therapy the doctor is recommending and, importantly, that the patient agrees with the goals you are both hoping to achieve.

Does this involve a screening tool, and what is it?

Yes, it does. Usually a K10 questionnaire (Kessler Psychological Distress Scale) or a DASS21 (Depression, Anxiety, Stress Survey) score, which the patient completes by answering questions. This doesn't diagnose – rather, it establishes a baseline. Improvement can then be monitored by repeating the test at a mental health review as early as three months later.

How does a mental health plan help?

The major advantage of these plans is that they enable the patient to access subsidised therapy from a psychologist.

Having done the mental health plan, the doctor can refer the patient for up to six subsidised sessions from a psychologist. The psychologist gets a Medicare rebate from the government for these sessions. If the patient completes all these six before twelve months pass, they can return to the GP and get a mental health review. The GP will review the original plan and check everything is on track. Then the doctor can refer for another four subsidised sessions, equating to ten visits a year. Of course, the patient can go more often – they just don't get the subsidy.

A mental health care plan should also include other treatments the patient might be undergoing, such as referral to a psychiatrist or any medication prescribed, but the patient can access these without a plan.

Is a mental health care plan all that is needed to address mental health concerns?

The mental health care plan is not an answer in itself. It is just a management tool, one that helps patients access psychological help; it has always been intended to support a team approach to treating mental illness.

What can someone do if they are worried about a loved one who doesn't want to seek help?

It is often so difficult for carers and parents and partners watching their loved one suffer a mental illness. As I say, once they get to a doctor or a psychologist, you're halfway there, but when they won't make or keep that appointment.

This is what I'd suggest:

- In Australia, try telehealth or online options.
- Lifeline and Beyond Blue have some great resources.
- Try the physical check-up approach and inform the doctor beforehand if needed.
- Set short-term, manageable goals, such as going out for coffee tomorrow morning, watching a TV series, and eating takeaway on Tuesdays.
- Try to get them to avoid exacerbating factors, such as excess alcohol.
- Try to promote healthy living. Diet and exercise won't cure mental illness, but they can help.

Chapter 15
Psychologist

A good psychologist will be happy to be interviewed by a potential patient by phone for five to ten minutes.

— Dr Amanda Ferguson

The role of a psychologist

Psychology studies human behaviour - how people experience emotions and sensations, and their actions and feelings. Psychologists have trained for up to six years, and also undertake ongoing learning and professional development. Their role is to investigate behaviour, assess, treat and counsel each client as an individual. Their goal is to describe, explain, predict, and help clients change their behaviour.

Chapter 16
Dr Amanda Ferguson's story: Psych for Life

Every time I hear a carer talk about their day-to-day life, I am grateful. People sharing their stories opens the door to discussion and educates all of us who listen. When Dr Amanda Ferguson invited me to chat on her podcast *Psych for Life*, I jumped at the opportunity, and when it came to speaking to a psychologist for *Dear Carer,* I knew who to ask. It was through talking to Dr Amanda that I realised how valuable it is to hear others' stories, so we can understand our own that bit more.

Dr Amanda, what happens when a new client has their initial appointment with you?

I will have already emailed the patient intake form to collect essential information that will help me to understand and help them. It sets out conditions, agreements and a detailed consent form, explaining how the information may be used and accessed. Psychologists aim to create a good rapport or 'therapeutic alliance' right from the beginning. If a patient doesn't experience this, the therapy is less likely to be effective.

Their GP, who likely referred them to a psychologist, will have already spoken to them about doing the DASS21 and the K10. If they have a mental health plan, they may have already done this.

People are often surprised to hear that their mood problems are not what they thought them to be. The treatment differs according to the indicators. I develop a treatment plan and provide resources as needed. The work can be anything from helping with problem-solving to being a safe sounding board, to helping people make fundamental changes in themselves and their lives. Often people will do a block of regular work with me to achieve what they require and then check in if needed over the decades afterwards.

I have heard accounts of people having a challenging time finding a psychologist who suits them. What would help in the process?

Getting a recommendation from your GP is a good start – most will have a list in their rooms. People can also find a psychologist on the internet. The Australian Psychological Society's 'Find a Psychologist' search portal is a good starting point. Once you have found a psychologist, call and make an appointment. A good psychologist will be happy to be interviewed by a potential patient by phone for five to ten minutes.

Sometimes people hear about a psychologist from friends or family members. It's important to check with the psychologist whether this would present a conflict of interest. Some psychologists have booking portal systems open to the public or provided privately once they are a patient.

Chapter 17
Psychiatrist

Try to establish a dialogue with the managing psychiatrist and or psychiatry registrar as soon as possible and ask to be informed of all major management issues.

— Professor Gordon Parker

The role of a psychiatrist

Psychiatrists are specialist medical doctors. Becoming a psychiatrist can take twelve to fifteen years of medical training, and education does not stop when specialist training finishes. Psychiatrists undertake ongoing learning throughout their working life. Their role is to assess, diagnose, and treat complex mental health conditions, and they collaborate with others to provide comprehensive medical care. As well as prescribing medication, they support and advocate for their patients. Psychiatrists work in hospitals, public and private practice, community services, and in inpatient and outpatient clinics.

Chapter 18
Professor Gordon Parker's story: Founding the Black Dog Institute

When I had almost finished my first book, *Dear Psychosis*, my husband lured me away from my writing to play golf. We arrived as a pair, but it's always better if another two players can join you. It also meant that we weren't stuck together for four hours, in the nicest possible way. Fortunately, another couple joined us.

We got to the seventh hole, and I was playing terribly. In fact, I wasn't sure if I would reach double figures on my scorecard, and that, my friends, is not great. I needed to make an excuse for my bad golf and said to the player walking beside me, 'Gordon. Sorry I'm playing so badly! I'm writing a book, and I have way too many ideas floating around in my brain. It's clearly distracting me'. I winked at him. He laughed, thank goodness. He asked me what I'd written, and I told him about *Dear Psychosis*. He then proceeded to ask me all the right questions. By now we were at the putting green, and I asked, 'Gordon, have you written a book?'

This man was Professor Gordon Parker AO – an eminent Australian psychiatrist and founder of the Black Dog Institute, which is a not-for-profit facility treating and diagnosing psychiatric conditions in Australia.

He is a big deal.

I was playing my worst ever golf with a gentleman who has written over twenty books on mental health. All I wanted to do was throw my golf clubs in the bushes and talk to this wonderful man about what he'd written, what I'd written, and all things mental health. At the end of the game, I asked if I could email him, and he kindly agreed. We still see each other at the golf course, and he doesn't run away or avoid me. He is kind and generous to a tee (all eighteen of them) and I feel fortunate to have met him. So, when it came time to write this book, I couldn't do it without talking with him.

In the 1980s, Gordon was appointed Head of the School of Psychiatry at Prince of Wales and Prince Henry Hospitals in Sydney, New South Wales. His first order of business was to set up and establish a clinical research facility, the Mood Disorders Unit. His team of psychiatrists accepted referrals from anybody in the state of New South Wales who were struggling with a mood disorder. The team's objective was to determine the correct diagnosis and its logical management. This was important to Gordon, as he felt that much of psychiatry was 'compromised by inaccurate and poor diagnoses', which commonly led to incorrect treatment.

Patients would come to the unit for an initial one or two hour consultation and assessment by an individual psychiatrist. Other psychiatrists would also interview new patients. The care team would then meet to discuss any patient concerns, to clarify issues, and determine the diagnosis and best management plan.

In addition to addressing the needs of patients, Gordon's team had a research function. With patients' permission, their data and experiences contributed to the team's research questions, such as how best to subtype depressive disorders, how to define melancholic depression, and how best to define bipolar disorders. These were the people who would not give up on the treatment and diagnosis of our loved ones. These were the people who were trying to find the next drug or treatment that might change people's lives.

Gordon felt the team operated on a 'win-win' model. The patients received a management plan and information, and the clinicians generated research data, allowing knowledge to advance. The team was thriving, and the facility was being recognised for the work coming out of it. They were the first Australian psychiatry group to be awarded a National Health and Medical Research Council Program Grant. The importance of this award meant that psychiatry was being recognised. I can only imagine the excitement that this would have caused and the ripple effect that resulted in the world of psychiatric mental health.

In its first ten years, the Mood Disorder Unit had assessed three thousand patients. Gordon was proud of his clinic's achievements, but he knew they could do more. He dreamed of a science and education institute with a particular interest in psychiatric conditions and psychiatric health.

Gordon implemented four components for this institute:

- Research
- Clinical service provision
- Education
- Community involvement.

The plan was that clinical observations would generate findings to be tested in research studies. If valid and important, findings would be fed into the educational programs and shared with the community. Gordon thought of naming the new entity 'The Mood Disorders Institute.' However, fellow board member Michael Eyers suggested 'The Black Dog Institute' – recognising Winston Churchill's description of his melancholic depression. A logo was developed with a hand splayed in the forefront giving the 'V for victory' gesture, creating a black dog in its shadow. The intended message was, 'we seek victory over depression but respect that depression can still shadow the sufferer.' If you head over to the Black Dog Institute website and have a look at the logo, it will bring new meaning and an aha moment when you see it.

For the institute to work, it needed reach. Gordon and his team contacted politicians and sportspeople to break the stigma and silence of psychiatric conditions by sharing their diagnoses with the community. Gordon approached John Konrads, a well-known Australian Olympic gold medal winning swimmer, who was also on the board of the Black Dog Institute, and asked if he'd be happy to talk to a Sydney newspaper about living with bipolar. Sometime after his interview, John was taking part in a community beach swim with hundreds of others. Unbeknownst to him, the article had been published that day. When he finished the swim, hundreds of people on the beach applauded him. Many had read the article and wanted to show their support for breaking the silence and sharing his personal mental health journey. That was the signal that many needed. Psychiatric conditions were not something to be afraid of. In fact, talking about it was the release that many needed.

The Black Dog Institute, Beyond Blue and SANE Australia ran campaigns in the early 2000s destigmatising psychiatric concerns. In fact, these campaigns had a significant impact on decreasing suicide over those years. Sadly, suicide rates have increased steadily since; no doubt we can and need to do more.

Gordon, how do Australians access psychiatry services?

In the public system, via the emergency department or in the private system via a referral process through your GP. For outpatient services, you can access a private psychiatrist if you are privately insured, otherwise the public system also offers outpatient services – with latter facilities based at public hospitals or community centres. Public and private tele-psychiatry services are an ever-increasing option and, if the assessing and managing psychiatrist is competent, this strategy has much to offer. It avoids lengthy commutes, and there is no hospital parking fee.

Are appointments with a psychiatrist covered by Medicare in Australia?

No cost is generally imposed in the public system. In the private system, the psychiatrist may accept the Medicare rebate only and thus not cost you any money, but nearly all will charge above the Medicare rebate – and to strikingly varying extents. It's important to ask about costs prior to an appointment. In fact, these should be stated at the time a booking is made.

Gordon, what advice do you have if hospitalisation is required?

Find out the 'driver' for hospitalisation (e.g. condition severity, suicide risk, violence risk). Try to establish a dialogue with the managing psychiatrist and or psychiatry registrar as soon as possible, and ask to be informed of all major management issues.

Visit your loved one regularly and offer support and hope. Be their advocate if they are facing serious issues. They may be unable to inform staff adequately if they are, for example, experiencing severe side-effects of a medication or being kept up all night by a patient in an adjacent bed.

What advice would you give to caregivers?

Seek the best information, be it from a health professional (GP, psychiatrist, psychologist) or from someone who has faced the same concerns or condition. Access reputed professional websites for salient diagnostic or management information about the condition in play. If you have concerns about the current management plan, seek a second professional opinion from someone with expertise in managing the particular condition.

Gordon, what do you do for your mental health?

Try to lower my golf handicap!

Chapter 19
The Prison Doctor

The role of a prison doctor

A doctor who works in the prison system has a vital role in an inmate's health. They are responsible for treating a variety of medical needs. Ranging from complex mental health, addiction, other chronic illnesses such as diabetes, kidney and heart disease to common coughs and colds. They also advocate for inmates within the jail to receive the best appropriate care. Prison doctors can work in collaboration with other health care professionals to provide the best medical care. When required patients can receive treatment outside of the jail environment.

Chapter 20
Dr Steven's story: healthcare in prison

The reception process will identify those with active current psychiatric conditions, and staff will rapidly refer cases of psychoses and disorganised thought to a psychiatric registrar or consultant.

— Dr Steven

Sadly, some of our loved ones living with complex mental health conditions commit criminal offenses and spend time in jail. I spoke with Dr Steven, who works at a maximum-security prison in Australia.

Dr Steven, what's the process when inmates come to prison?

In the state I practice in, all individuals will be seen by a medical doctor, registered nurse, prisoner liaison officer, and Indigenous liaison officer, if Aboriginal or Torres Strait Islander, within twenty-four hours of arrival to the prison. This is routine, and important to note that the law requires receiving all inmates within twenty-four hours of arrival. Most psychiatric crises have started before someone is admitted into the prison – this can sometimes be a contributing factor to their arrest.

If an individual is psychotic, they are treated by a psychiatrist and given medication. As a prison doctor, I don't review psychotic patients unless they have other medical issues as well.

For prisoners in the general prison population, going to see the prison doctor is via self-referrals from inmates; urgent reviews, via staff who may have observed strange actions or behaviours, an injury or perhaps self-harm; medical codes, such as someone collapsing or experiencing chest pain; and other emergencies. Officers can sometimes tell that someone is sick and may ask us to see them. Or there might be an injury the inmate might not tell us about, but a guard or other inmate might notice.

Some inmates may be in the police jail cells for multiple days, awaiting sentencing or due to a specific court delay. In the police cells, they would receive minimal psychiatric attention. If they have a psychiatric break, they will be moved to prison as soon as possible, or they will be taken to the emergency department of the nearest public hospital.

When seen by the prison doctor, patients with psychiatric needs are given a mental health risk rating: P1, P2, P3, or P4.

P1 is a serious psychiatric condition requiring intensive or immediate care.
P2 is a significant or ongoing psychiatric condition requiring psychiatric treatment.
P3 is a stable psychiatric condition requiring an appointment or continuing treatment.
P4 is a suspected psychiatric condition requiring assessment.

If someone needs to be seen during a normal week within the prison, there is a triage and clinic system. Mental health nurses will conduct reviews throughout the clinic all day. This means that those with current active psychiatric issues will be seen by a psychiatrist as soon as possible.

Those with current psychoses, or with behavioural issues of the highest order, will be in a specific prison that has the ability to hold P1 patients. This means safe cells, single cells with constant monitoring. Following triage, the psychiatric team will decide how often reviews are needed. Welfare checks can happen frequently. Anyone with current suicidal thoughts or intentions will be under appropriate monitoring, such as visual observations and speaking with them.

When self-referring, the patient will write on a form what their issue is, and the relevant teams will read and triage. Officers can also voice their concern about someone's mental health – they will particularly pick up on behavioural changes, self-harm, mood changes, etc.

What happens when someone goes to jail and has complex mental health conditions but is undiagnosed?

The reception process will identify those with active current psychiatric conditions, and staff will rapidly refer cases of psychoses and disorganised thought to a psychiatric registrar or consultant. Those with more insidious issues, like a major depression that may make them seem flat (which is normal when arriving to prison) may be harder to pick up – as in the community, it is difficult to estimate true self-harm risk at any time.

What is the process if my loved one has a complex mental health condition? Are they placed with the general population?

Yes – unless they are considered a risk to themselves or others. As above, if they have an active psychiatric condition with psychosis or severely disorganised thought, delusions, etc, they may be placed in a psychiatric-specific unit, depending on which prison they are in. If they are considered of the highest risk, they will be classified as a P1 and placed in a specific unit with safe cells. These patients will be moved from satellite prisons to central ones that have these facilities.

How are medications given?

If someone is in the general prison population, they will line up at their designated medication administration times. Most prisons will only do twice-daily dosing for the general population. If they are in a psychiatric-specific unit or at-risk unit, the mental health nurses will administer all medicines to ensure compliance.

What if medication is refused?

This depends. Similarly to outside of jail, with treatment orders, they may be changed to a depot injection. The medication in these injections is designed to be released into the body over an extended period, maintaining a consistent drug level. This is of use if medication is required but the person is refusing to take it. Regarding medical care outside of treatment orders, inmates may refuse any medicine that I, the medical doctor, might prescribe, just as on the outside.

Dr Steven, what's your advice around who families should speak to if they have concerns about their loved one's health during their incarceration?

There is a complete lack of control for the families in this instance – which is always going to be hard to accept. Families can help by being organised, having the most recent psychiatric and medical letters, including instructions for medications. Otherwise, the teams will generally get these from the doctors with release of information requests.

Who to talk to would be prison specific. In short, though, it's going to be hard. I believe that the psychiatric teams do have contact with some family members. There have been times I have reviewed patients due to family concern, but generally families will need to rely on the medical and psychiatric systems in place.

What do you do for self-care?

Hobbies and socialising, primarily. Debriefing and philosophy, if anything needs reflection.

Chapter 21
Allied Health Care

Allied health workers work within a multidisciplinary team to provide specialised treatment and support for our loved ones in an inpatient or outpatient setting.

— Sarah

When my elderly father spent eight weeks in public hospital after an operation, the nurses spoke to us about the allied health team. Having worked as a peri-operative nurse, I didn't think there was anything unusual about this but my spouse, who works in information technology, had zero clue what allied health meant.

What does the term 'allied health' mean?

Allied health professionals encompass a broad spectrum of people who deliver care in hospital, outpatient services, and aged care facilities. Their role is to diagnose, provide treatment, promote health and prevent illness, aid in recovery, and to provide advice on preventative care.

Allied health describes accredited health professionals who are not doctors, nurses or dentists. They work within multidisciplinary teams in inpatient or outpatient settings, in the public and private sectors, providing specialised treatment and support for our loved ones.

It's important that if we don't know what someone's role is, no matter who they are, that we ask questions.

- What their position or job title is.
- What they can do to help our loved one or us as a carer.

Who exactly are allied health professionals?

Some examples are:

- Psychologists, counsellors and psychotherapists.
- Physiotherapists, exercise physiologists, and chiropractors.
- Occupational therapists.
- Social workers.
- Dietitians.
- Peer workers.
- Art and music therapists.
- Audiologists and speech pathologists.
- Pharmacists.
- Podiatrists.

The multidisciplinary team setting is important for allied health professionals. They collaborate and create shared goals prioritised by your loved one. If your loved one shares information about their life and medical journey, the team can incorporate it into the bigger picture to focus on the most appropriate treatment for them.

Allied health professionals work in the private hospital system as well as the public. I have had people tell me that they had no idea there was a physiotherapist, dietitian or other such allied health workers available in the private system. Please ask your specialist or nurse unit manager if you or your loved one would like to be referred to, for instance, a social worker or psychologist.

When talking with any medical personnel, be specific with questions. Write them down prior to meeting with staff. It's not rude to take notes - I always make staff aware when I take notes, as it's an important way to avoid forgetting what's said. You can also ask to record the conversation to refer to at a later time. You don't have to do this, but I find when relaying information to my family that it is the most accurate. Plus, I don't forget what information I have received, as it can be overwhelming when there is information overload.

Some information on three allied health roles

Let me tell you about three common allied health roles: social worker, occupational therapist, and dietitian.

Chapter 22
Social worker

Social workers partner with people to help them address personal difficulties and structural barriers in their lives. They provide tools to build better support for those who may be facing health, economic, and social issues. Their aim is to assess the circumstances, develop a care plan, and connect our loved one with the most appropriate resources. Ultimately, they are there to understand people in the context of their lives, and identify the root causes of distress to determine the best support.

Social workers advocate, counsel, case manage, educate, and mediate if needed, to assist those who need help to function effectively. They focus on social issues, advocate for the rights of our loved ones, and promote positive change. Social workers can help navigate the public and private health systems, access information and add to the existing care plan in the medical notes.

In a private hospital setting, involvement is usually session-based and funded through Medicare, private health insurance and/or the National Disability Insurance Scheme. It is more counselling focused. In a public setting, there is more access to multidisciplinary teams, hospital systems and case coordination.

Chapter 23
Pi's story: social work in mental health

I spoke with Pi to understand how social workers help our loved ones.

Pi, what is the role of a social worker?

Social workers can step in at the point of diagnosis, during admission, when information becomes overwhelming. We can support the carer to navigate the hospital and medical system. This can be especially important when there's a break in communication between services, or when risks increase, such as self-harm, or the deterioration of your loved one. Family conflict is another challenge we can support you to manage. We also have a significant role to play when your loved one disengages from services.

What do social workers do in their initial assessment?

We will do a social work assessment that involves looking at social and physiological factors that affect someone's health. We'll also ask questions such as, 'why did you have this problem at this time?' and we can do a treatment plan and recommend actions that can decrease future risk, and plan assessments in the future. These assessments can assist us in determining what direction of care and education is required for your loved one and those caring for them.

Advocacy seems to be a big part of social work.

Definitely. We will advocate for your loved one and you, the carer, to ensure appropriate delivery of services or therapy. This may include following up on delayed appointments, communicating with GPs around scripts or referrals, or alerting teams to deteriorating mental health and helping carers being heard in meetings. Our aim is to work towards independence and the resolution of any crises that have occurred. An example of this may be facilitating conflict resolution between family services.

Chapter 24
Occupational therapist

Occupational therapists (OT) aid our loved one's recovery and help them develop the skills needed for day-to-day life. They educate families and caregivers about treatment plans. Their goal is to get our loved ones discharged from the hospital and working towards independence. Their care is patient-centred and includes assessment, intervention, and discharge planning when in hospital.

How can they help?

OTs help with daily living skills needed for independence, including using technology, dressing, cooking, personal hygiene, and mobility. They work with our loved ones to practise doing the things they need and like to do each day. They collaborate with other mental health care workers to provide a comprehensive care plan specific to our loved ones. They monitor and document progress and tweak any plans that are needed.

Chapter 25
Dietitian

As research continues to show us how important our gut and internal health is, dietitians have become key members in the mental health space. Diet plays a vital role in our mental and physical health, regardless of whether we are ill.

Medications can have significant side effects and, as carers, we are aware of the impact these have on our loved ones' bodies. Common side effects, like weight gain and lethargy, can contribute to ongoing mental health struggles. Dietitians collaborate with you and your loved one, and also work with other mental health care professionals and allied health staff.

Chapter 26
Georgie's story: diet and mental health

I can't write about the role of a dietitian without talking about hospital food. Honestly ... it's not the best! Many visitors and carers bring loved ones food from home or fast food. I spoke to Georgie, a dietitian who works at a large public hospital, about why we need to be cautious around food, not just fast food

Georgie, hospital food isn't the best. How can we help our loved ones eat well in hospital?

I hear what you're saying about food and hospitals. Let's talk about the realistic options that are available.

If it is a meal, bring it in at mealtime, not in between. If you opt for less healthy choices, choose smaller portions. Provide delicious, in-season fruit like mangoes, dragon fruit, berries, or kiwifruit.

Boredom is often a precursor to eating. Having alternatives available is a great idea. Read to your loved one, and encourage creative outlets like painting or drawing, or problem solving like puzzles or sudoku.

Dear Carer,

Food can often be used as an emotional crutch. Can dietitians help our loved ones find alternative food choices?

Food can be emotive. We also need to realise that food is not always the solution to our emotional responses. Exercise and sunshine can positively affect mood and motivation. Inpatients can go for a walk around the hospital grounds or around the unit. Outpatients can go for a bush or beach walk, or a wander around the area where you live. A change of scenery is small, but for someone who hasn't left the house or hospital room for a while, it can be significant.

What kind of education regarding diet can dietitians provide?

As dietitians, we work hard to educate regarding:

- Portions
- Healthy eating
- Re-engaging with the body's signals of hunger and fullness
- Working with occupational therapists to help with cooking classes, budgeting and meal planning.

There's a lot of evidence around the Mediterranean diet leading to decreased signs and symptoms of anxiety and depression, and connecting the gut health - brain axis.

Chapter 27
Care Plans

As care plans have been mentioned several times over the last few pages, I think now is a good time to clarify what they are and what they do.

What is a care plan?

A care plan is a formal document that outlines the specific care required for an individual (in this case, our loved one). There are a number of teams looking after our loved one while in hospital and as an outpatient as well. This can mean there might be a number of care plans in operation at the same time. Communication between teams is important to ensure plans don't contradict each other. Here, I will focus on care plans from a nursing perspective.

Nursing care plans address:

- Diagnosis.
- Goals and outcomes.

- Interventions.
- Evaluation.

Care plans should:

- Be individual and person centred, led by your loved one (if they are able to articulate their goals).
- Document personal needs.
- Outline goals that are achievable and empowering.
- Support trauma-informed care and be recovery focussed.
- Provide for continual updates.
- Include the carer's perspective.

Care plans can be described in lay terms as being similar to when you join a gym and the fitness instructor asks you about your goals and how you expect to get there; it's a joint effort between you and the fitness team. Similarly, there is continual monitoring on any fitness journey, and it is expected that you will change anything that doesn't work to something that does.

Why our loved ones should have a care plan

A care plan is (or should be) a collaboration with our loved ones, their medical team and nominated carer. It is a document that is in every patient's medical notes. In fact, carer input is essential if it can be provided. As a carer, if you have not been asked for input, then please ask the nursing unit manager for their care plan documentation and related standards (these standards may differ between states in Australia).

Care plans improve clear and concise communication between our loved one and the medical team. They enhance continuity of care during every shift or change of staff.

Chapter 28
Partner Care

Establishing a crisis or action plan when life is stable can bring comfort and reassurance.

— Sarah

N*ote: If you are reading 'Partner Care' as a stand-alone chapter, please refer to 'Early Care' and 'Emergency Care' as well.*

It would be remiss not to add a chapter specifically for partners. You might live with your partner, or live separately but take on the caring role. If you have concerns that your partner is unwell, start talking about it. These discussions may take place over days, weeks or months. Plant the seeds and let them grow.

Living with complex mental health means that control and decision making may be out of your loved one's hands. Making decisions together is great, and including ideas that your loved one has come up with themselves is an absolute bonus. Establishing an action plan when life is stable, before it's needed, can bring comfort and reassurance.

Dear Carer,

Be aware that your partner may be resistant to seeking or receiving help when it's needed. Try to remember that what looks like help to you, may not look or feel like help to your partner. Many people lack insight into their illness and struggle to acknowledge that they have a mental health condition. There may be a few reasons for this response. Could it be based in fear? If so, what can be done to ease this? Talking to your GP with your loved one can help, as they may shed some light on the situation. If your loved one is at risk to themselves or others, seek emergency care immediately.

Talking with your partner about their mental health can be stressful and confronting

If this is the first time that the topic of mental health has been broached then I reiterate that you and your partner speak with a trusted person such as your GP, counsellor, psychologist or psychiatrist. There is always the possibility that your loved one does not have the capacity to be involved in these conversations. This can be confronting and scary, but it does not mean that your loved one can't add their insights in the future. Remember, you are a team.

Build your own toolkit

Finances

- When are the bills and/or rent due?
- If you have a mortgage or other debt, how much is owed and when are repayments due?
- Keep track of incoming invoices and payments
- Do you require a weekly or monthly budget?
- Separate bank accounts. One with everyday spending money and the other with savings

- Bank accounts that need both your and your partner's passwords to remove money from the account.

Legalities

- Power of attorney and enduring guardianship
- Current wills
- Life insurance
- Superannuation
- Income protection.

Boundaries

- What is negotiable and non-negotiable to maintain emotional safety.
- Personal space and self care.

Feelings and emotions within the family unit

These can be hard to articulate and manage. What can we put in place so that, as a family, we can know that behaviour may be changing? The obvious is stating how we feel out loud, but this can get old quickly – I've tried it and it was annoying for all our family. If you have children living at home, they may find it more realistic to share how they're feeling by showing it rather than saying the words.

Perhaps have coloured bracelets made, or a chart on the fridge with coloured magnets. This can be used and changed multiple times a day. All the members of the family can join in. You can simplify the words to describe what each colour means depending on the age of the children. Your loved one might actually appreciate that everyone is wearing a wristband. Now, this may be used more as an early intervention tool rather than in crisis. It can normalise conversations about feelings and foster awareness within your family.

. . .

It may look like this:

Red - help is needed.
Orange – Angry. Overwhelmed. I need space.
Yellow – Lets talk. I'm fine. Just tired.
Green – all good.
Blue – feeling sad, depressed and tired.

You can choose your own colours and words to go with each wrist band or item you choose to wear. Come up with other themes that work for you as a family.

Living with complex mental health, as you know, doesn't just affect your loved one, it affects you and your children too. It's always a positive to check in and chat with your children. I've personally found car rides – to and from school or weekend sport – a wonderful time to chat. Some rides may be filled with silence, but others are lined with gold – when the magic happens and discussions flow.

Things to do during a mental health episode or crisis

Your safety and that of your family are the most important. If your partner is showing signs of psychosis, or risky or threatening behaviour, it is important to call emergency services. This can be scary and stressful, and your partner may not want you to – but it is the best course of action for everybody's safety.

Your loved one may not understand that you cannot see or hear what they are seeing or hearing. This may lead to extreme frustration, which may turn into anger and violence. If this is the case, you need to remove yourself from the situation immediately and call emergency services.

Know your partner's emotional responses. If one of their known reactions is to emergency services, specifically police or paramedics, let the operator know. This may mean police or paramedics arrive without lights and sirens.

Driving your partner to the emergency department may be an alternative to calling emergency services. Either way, hospital is the safest place for them.

Things to do after this crisis or episode is over

I have written when 'this' episode is over because, like with any chronic illness, mental ill-health can return. It brings with it a lifelong vigilance.

If possible, have an open and honest conversation with your partner about what the experience was like for them, and for you. Think about what worked and what didn't, and what you might try differently next time. Add these to your toolkit.

Surround yourself with people who can assist you and your family. Think about whether you are comfortable sharing critical medical information, and who with. Do friends, day care, teachers, or work colleagues need to know? Talk anonymously with others on mental health forums. Here you will receive more information for your toolkit. Chat with a counsellor or psychologist. There are many free options out there, and I implore you to not live through this alone.

Lastly don't forget self care. It is a precious thing that we can do for us, in the now, to recharge our batteries. Caring brings stress and strain. The importance of looking after *you* cannot be talked about enough. Think about when you last had time out just for you. Perhaps now is the time to book that outing, golf trip or holiday.

Self care doesn't need to be time consuming or expensive. Sitting outside for half an hour, alone with a cup of tea, can help you gather your energy to get through the rest of the day. A YouTube yoga session can help you reconnect to your body and find a sense of calm. The important thing is to make space for rest and recovery, so you can continue to be available to support your partner and family.

Dear Carer,

Restore. Recharge. Revitalise. The three R's you need in your life. Oh, and leave any guilt you may have at the door on your way out.

Chapter 29
Gemma's story: caring for a partner

The small things DO add up and ultimately make a difference.

— Gemma

I have had the pleasure of chatting with Gemma over the last year. We share a love of the open air, talking, reading and, of course, mental health. She mentioned that she would be happy to share her family's story, 'if I would like.' I couldn't say yes fast enough!

Relationships ... no two are the same. Hearing from someone whose partner lives with complex mental health is important. My thanks to Gemma, who opened her door and allowed us in.

Can you share with us how complex mental health entered your life?

Several years ago, my partner of twenty years experienced a catastrophic event in his workplace that had an immediate and profound effect on his life. Despite doing all the recommended things

– taking time off, seeking counselling, and consulting with medical and psychology services, his mental health deteriorated steadily, and then rapidly over the course of several months. Eventually, he suffered a terrifying 'breakdown' requiring hospital admission and emergency mental health care that undoubtedly saved his life.

Following this, my partner was not the same person. He was unable to recall certain memories, including much of the high-level technical skills and knowledge he had utilised in his career prior to this event. It was clear from the outset that he would never be able to return to his job. The official diagnosis was post-traumatic stress disorder (PTSD), complicated by a neurodiverse brain – which, we subsequently found out, processes trauma differently to that of a neurotypical brain.

As well as the debilitating anxiety, which at times bordered on psychosis and paranoia, my partner experienced uncontrollable flashbacks, disorientation to the point of passing out, frequent episodes of distress and overwhelm, a complete blow-out of executive functioning and an extreme sensitivity to stress.

Did having your children at home make things harder?

With two primary school aged children in the home, I quickly had to pick up and hold together many pieces of family and household life. I was handling my own loss and grief about what had happened, as well as processing real concerns about the impact this would have on our lives as a couple and as a family.

Gemma, do you think of yourself as a carer?

Over the last few years, my experience as a 'carer' has been as complex as my partner's mental health. The reason I put 'carer' in inverted commas is because there has always been something about the term that doesn't sit quite right with me! Reflecting on it, I realise this is my own inner prejudice, as I seem to only be able to think of

Florence Nightingale-type figures who tirelessly do things for the subject in their care, with no expectation of getting anything back. This is not me, and I daresay this is not realistic or sustainable for anyone, really – at least not without buckets of insight and support. Even then, the cost is likely to be high.

For me, caring for my partner has predominantly been about allowing him to take the space and time required to heal, and to walk alongside him as his friend while he does this. It has been about knowing when to lean in and when to step back. It has been about creating routines and patterns that are predictable so as not to cause any unnecessary mental load. This can be as simple as having the same meals on the same night every week – something I hate because it isn't spontaneous, but that takes the pressure off having to think on your feet. Thinking and planning can be hard when you have complex mental health considerations in the family unit. Basic life admin can turn into a nightmare to be avoided at all costs. It can take a lot of time and patience to complete what seems like a simple task.

Have you been impacted financially by not having both of you working?

Financial and legal stressors have been a massive component of my capacity to function within this situation. I cannot emphasise this enough. Originally, the relief of having a workers compensation scheme as a safety net took enormous pressure off us. We could focus on the immediate mental health concerns and needs of our family without the burden of worrying about bills. However, the inevitable machinations of the compensation process meant that in the long-term, with evidence of a lifelong injury, we had to ultimately confront a lengthy and extraordinarily complex process of legal negotiations.

There is a lot of research about the impact of workers compensation schemes on mental health and wellness that I won't recount here, but from firsthand experience, going through this process has undoubtedly compounded my partner's trauma and impaired his recovery. The vicarious trauma I have also experienced as a result of going through this process with him is hard to measure, but it is real, and I have my own set of psychological symptoms and triggers around security as a result.

This is why I want to make the point that, as a carer, the peace of mind that comes from making sure your financial and legal situation is taken care of as much as possible is a significant help. It is one less thing to think about. For example, at one point I received a grant from Carers Gateway NSW to pay for my part of our will to be done. When I did the intake assessment with them, they recognised that I was at financial risk due to the unpredictability of my partner's health. They suggested that having my legal affairs in order was prudent. It was a lot of work, but such a relief to get it done.

Over the past year alone, I have consulted with a financial advisor through a local charity who helped me with a budget. I have consulted with family lawyers at Legal Aid; and I have specifically requested appointments with a social worker at Centrelink to help work out benefits and get general advice. I have found all these people to be incredibly helpful.

Gemma, what changes have you noticed within your partner?

One of the things that has struck me is that he finds it hard to see positive growth and evidence of change. One of the important things I do is try to reflect with him on how far we all have come.

It is hard not to make this sound condescending, but sometimes it is about voicing appreciation that 'hey – there was no way you could have handled this six months ago,' or 'yep, that paperwork was pretty full-on, but look, it's finally done! Now can we please go out for dinner?'

Is it hard having conversations about the future?

Sometimes there is a need for deeper conversations with a partner because there is so much room for resentment to build about the things that we could have, would have, should have been doing if this hadn't happened.

Our reality looks quite different from what we may have envisioned for ourselves. This is where it is important to have someone to talk to – a counsellor or a group of trusted friends. This can help to gain insight into how life is different but also acknowledge that there are positives to uncover. Goals can be changed, things can be looked at differently. Hopefully there will be people in your life who will readily adapt to the changes that complex mental health situations can bring. These people will be happy to come alongside you and have the conversation.

Do you have any advice or tips you would like to share?

I heard once that people are generally happy to accommodate the 'someone gets sick and then they get better' model, but it takes a different kind of person to accommodate the 'someone gets unwell, they get better for a bit, they get worse again, they get stuck, plateau, get a bit better and so on.' This is a quite different picture. The paradigm has changed. The important people in your life and community will hopefully be able to adjust. If they can't, then maybe they are not that helpful right now.

What I have learned is that unmet needs will fester if they are not opened up and dealt with. Sometimes there needs to be a conversation – something along the lines of 'hey, to feel loved by you I need this to happen.' I once read in *The Five Love Languages*, a book by Gary Chapman, that part of loving someone is finding out what that person needs to feel that they are cared about – and then making an effort to do it!

If you are predominantly the carer in your relationship, it doesn't mean that your loved one gets off the hook with this. I have also learned the hard way that conversations about expectations need to happen with both partners.

The partner with complex mental health may or may not be aware that they feel pressured by real, external, or imagined expectations about how they should be managing and what they should be doing. The partner in the caring role may need to examine what expectations they have of their partner, and whether this is realistic or achievable. It needs to be addressed if expectations are unclear or are not being met. Couples counselling may be helpful with this.

Parenting school-aged children, in addition to having a partner with complex mental health brings its own challenges. Communication is key. I have learned that serious conversations about family, or anything I am not happy about, need to occur in a certain way and at a certain pace. I am learning to take a step back and text my partner to give him a heads-up or ask if it's a good time to have a certain conversation. Then give him a run-down of any agenda I have, so that he has time to process his thoughts and opinions.

Not doing this can lead to conflict because he feels blindsided by surprise conversations, especially if I am emotional or have a problem that needs to be worked through. Similarly, we have an understanding in our family that everyone has their bandwidth, and we all need to tap out at certain times. These expressions are understood by us all, and we are learning to respect them.

It is definitely not perfect, and we absolutely have our share of bad days and family tension. I feel proud that our children are learning to be thoughtful about their interactions, and that they are learning to take time out for themselves when they recognise that they need it.

Do you have a mental health plan in place?

Yes. We have a crisis plan in place that I review fairly regularly with our children. They know how and when to get help from neighbours, family friends and emergency services.

They know how to recognise when their father is having a bad head day, and they understand that it's not personal because we have explained why he experiences these symptoms. We use humour a lot in our interactions with our children, and I like to reflect with them on points of connection.

I used to feel overwhelmed thinking that family life had to be a wonderful experience all the time, which was completely unrealistic! Now I am content if I can get to the end of the day and reflect on a handful of occasions, or even just one, where I have had a good point of connection with each one of them. This might be a nice chat over dinner, a card game or a shared joke.

The small things DO add up and ultimately make a difference.

Chapter 30
Trauma-Informed Care

Trauma-informed care assists in advocacy as it pays attention to a person's experience and how this might be impacting the present, rather than just looking at a person through a biomedical model or through a generic, diagnosis-only lens.

— Aliceson

What is trauma-informed care?

Trauma-informed care recognises and is responsive to the impact of trauma on someone's life. It is a strengths-based approach, recognising survival and resilience. It emphasises safety, trust, choice, collaboration, and empowerment. Trauma-informed care in the mental health space creates opportunities for people with complex mental health concerns to regain a sense of purpose and identity. It helps services and clinicians to understand the unique aspects of people's experiences, and to create a space for physical and psychological healing.

As carers, we have much to learn in the ever-changing space of mental and psychiatric health. Many of our loved ones live with trauma. Trauma-informed care acknowledges that past trauma can still have a big impact on the present. It forms part of the everyday plan that health care workers use to care for our loved ones. As Trish, our mental health nurse, put it, 'Implementing trauma-informed care has been essential ... it will make an enormous difference in patient outcomes when we consider the patient's history and how best to approach and engage. I would say most mental health clinicians implement trauma-informed care into their practice daily.'

Trauma-informed care is a relatively new development in the mental health space. It is an enormous step in the right direction. Rather than being asked, 'what's wrong with you?' people are now asked, 'what has happened to get you here?'

Taking the time to ask questions without making assumptions is a positive step forward. Medical personnel holding space for our loved one to answer questions in their own words – not speaking for them, or putting words in their mouths – is all part of trauma informed care. Importantly, your loved one is part of the health care team.

Chapter 31
Aliceson's story: trauma-informed care in public health

To learn more about trauma informed care, I spoke with Aliceson, a clinician in the public health system.

Aliceson, can you tell us about trauma-informed care?

Trauma-informed care is a holistic and strengths-based approach. It considers the system of care and support a consumer exists in and the interdependent relationships they may have. Collaboration with these key people is essential in working with the whole person.

How does trauma-informed care help carers?

Trauma-informed care assists in advocacy as it pays attention to a person's experience and how this might be impacting the present, rather than just looking at a person through a biomedical model or through a generic, diagnosis only lens. It also recognises how families and carers might be affected, and the potential strengths in these support networks.

I do think it is terminology that gets bandied around a lot, and perhaps co-opted by services just to use the language with no real implications for how services are delivered. It is my deep conviction to be a part of making sure this isn't the case; to create systems and structures for true understanding and accountability.

Trauma-informed care is a welcome and much-needed initiative in the mental health space.

There is a lot of work in this space at a national, state and local level, including communities of practice and service development initiatives. The Agency for Clinical Innovation's *Trauma-informed care in mental health services across NSW: A framework for change* is a recently developed resource for individuals and services to grow in a trauma-informed care approach.

There are many ways of working that are underpinned by trauma-informed care, such as the Hearing Voices movement, and Blue Knot. Recovery-oriented, trauma-informed clinicians will be supporting the consumer to lead their recovery, and this will include advocacy or supported advocacy as someone works towards self-advocacy.

The most important part of advocacy is hearing from those with lived experience, as it sits at the centre of advocacy. It must lead all aspects of an individual's journey as well as the broader mental health service design, development and delivery. How can support and service provision exist if they don't consider the needs and perspectives of those it exists for?

Can you share your 'why' – the reason you decided to work in the mental health field?

I had a wonderful university placement in occupational therapy and mental health that ignited my curiosity and interest in complex mental health. I found the breadth of human experience and ways of coping fascinating, and I saw the impact of an occupational therapy lens in this space. So I sought to work in this area once I graduated. I entered with the expectation of all I could contribute and the professional expertise I could bring to fix the problems.

Now, I think, how naïve and arrogant this was! In contrast, I have discovered the humbling privilege it is to walk alongside people and to have learnt so much from them – about myself, about the human experience, and about so much more. I did not expect to be so transformed in my understanding, perspective and way of being as a clinician.

Lastly, what would you tell your younger self?

There is so much to learn! You are going to have the privilege of getting to know and journey alongside so many incredible people. You will be invited into sacred spaces of despair and pain, along with growth and joy. You will be exposed to injustices and power imbalances that will fuel a conviction and passion for activism and change.

You will have unexpected teachers, away from textbooks and learned experts. People who will challenge you, shine a light on your judgements and flawed ways of thinking, show you grace and broaden your perspective. It will be hard and confusing, and sometimes you will need to learn to let go of ego, power, and control. There will be a lot of unlearning to be done, but the re-learning and rebuilding will be energising and fulfilling.

You will be forever changed. You will let go of knowing and certainty, be comfortable with simply being present, and you will keep learning to listen deeply and be led by those most impacted.

Chapter 32
Suicide Care

How do you know what people ... need, unless you have heard from them?

— Bronwen

I am grateful for the input and wisdom from Bronwen Edwards – founder and CEO of Roses in the Ocean – in writing this chapter on suicide care.

For many, the word *suicide* is frightening and may be distressing. It can arrive quietly, in a passing comment, or come headfirst into us without warning. This chapter is for anyone who has experienced any aspect of suicide – living with suicidal thoughts, having made an attempt on your life, supported a loved one through crisis or after an attempt, or experienced the death of someone through suicide.

This chapter is not here to make you an expert or to scare you, but to help you feel less alone, less afraid, and more supported as you walk alongside someone you love who is considering if they can stay connected with life. It is here to enable you to speak when necessary, to hold space when needed, and to reach out to those who can assist.

Dear Carer,

Talking about suicide with someone you trust – a close friend or a health professional – may be your first port of call. Educating yourself about suicide, attending suicide intervention skills training, and reading and listening to stories of other people who have a lived experience of suicide are also helpful actions for you to take. The more you understand, the more support you can offer to the person who needs you.

Please note that resources can be found in the 'Links to Resources' section at the end of the book.

How do we support someone with suicidal thoughts?

We often talk about holding space. This means being fully present. We can hold space by creating a safe space to talk, having a nonjudgmental conversation, allowing emotions to come into play and hearing the words that your loved one is saying. This is vital when we know or suspect that someone is having suicidal thoughts. Remember, not everyone who has suicidal thoughts will act on them. But mentions of suicide or self harm should always be taken seriously. If you are concerned, don't be afraid to start a conversation.

Before you initiate this kind of conversation, consider whether you have the capacity to talk about specific mental health concerns or to discuss subjects such as suicide. If you are worried about someone's immediate safety, call emergency services.

Make the call

Don't hesitate. Call.

In an emergency call 000.
Lifeline 13 11 14
Suicide text back service 0477 13 11 14
Beyond Blue 1300 224 636

13 YARN 13 92 76 (Aboriginal and Torres Strait Islander crisis support).
QLife 1800 184 527 (LGBTQIA peer support).
Befrienders worldwide (Global suicide prevention) https://www.befrienders.org

Always be transparent with the person who is experiencing distress and get their consent before making arrangements to speak with anyone else. If this all sounds like it is too much to cope with, ring Lifeline or any other help lines. Roses in the Ocean has information on lived experience with suicide, one of the topics they discuss is how to hold open discussions with others regarding suicide.

How do I know if someone is unwell or thinking of suicide?

It is to be noted that you may not see any sign that anything is different or that behaviour has changed. But you may be aware of small changes or actions, you may notice very subtle invitations for help or warning signs

Recognising changes in behaviour like:

- Suddenly happy and content.
- Giving things away.

You may read between the lines, or feel something is 'off' with your loved one or friend. Are they:

- talking about wanting to die.
- talking about guilt or shame.
- talking about being a burden.
- eating less or eating more.
- sleeping less or sleeping more.
- increasing their drug and/or alcohol intake.

These may indicate a range of troubles, but if you suspect that suicide is in someone's thoughts – say the words, start a conversation. Ask the person directly:

- how they are.
- are they thinking of harming themselves?
- are they thinking of suicide, planning suicide or do they have suicidal thoughts?

Say those words.

But if I say the word 'suicide' ... is that going to make my loved one choose suicide?

Asking someone if they are having suicidal thoughts or planning suicide is not going to make them act. Don't be afraid to start a conversation. If your loved one has been thinking about or planning suicide, it's time to sit and listen – really listen without judgement. If the answer to questions about suicide is 'yes,' the important thing is that the person is validated. It takes strength and vulnerability for them to share that they are struggling; tell them how proud you are of them for sharing this journey with you.

You can then work with them to decide what type of support they would like. You can help them to reach out to health professionals, or call a helpline like Lifeline or Roses in the Ocean's Peer CARE companion call back service (this is for non-crisis support only.) If they or you are concerned for their immediate safety, then discuss with them about calling emergency services.

Don't forget, it's important that you seek support for yourself if needed. See the 'Self care' chapter for suggestions and more information.

What if a loved one refuses help?

Sometimes our loved ones cannot see or understand how unwell they are, leading them to refuse help. This can leave you feeling scared, frustrated, frightened, bewildered, and guilty.

It is important to call emergency services if someone talks of harming themselves or others. This can be a vital way to help them in an acute crisis. Being transparent and honest with someone talking about suicide is important. Collaborating with them regarding the next step is a positive outcome.

Feeling guilty

Many carers, friends and loved ones live with guilt. For what they missed, what they said or did, or what they did not say or do. As much as we want it, none of us hold that magic wand of healing. Keep advocating, keep loving, keep being you. But importantly, don't forget to look after yourself. Guilt does not mean you failed; it means that you cared deeply.

Please do not go through this grief alone. Griefline is free, and experienced operators are waiting for your call. Phone a friend and simply say, '*I need you.*' Helplines, forums and health professionals are not just for our loved ones ... they are for us, too.

As a carer, how do we talk about what's happening with children, tweens and teens?

Some kids can sense when something is wrong in the home, even when we try and protect them from it. Other kids may be oblivious to what's going on right in front of them. There is a choice to make ... to share or not to share. Every child is different and you know your child the best.

Honest, age-appropriate conversations help reduce fear and

confusion, especially if there are closed-door conversations and whispered talks with relatives or friends. You do not need to share everything. Share enough for them to feel safe and supported. Remember to ask if anything is worrying them or if they have any questions. Make an appointment with a health professional with your children.

Roses in the Ocean

In 2008, Bronwen Edwards' brother, Mark, died by suicide. He was a young man who had served his country as an RAAF fighter pilot and later as a commercial pilot. A few weeks after his death, the family went to Mark's favourite beach to place roses in the ocean, to celebrate his life. They spoke with the children in their families to make sure that they knew that being sad or struggling didn't mean that you would die.

Bronwen recognised a need to break the silence and stigma surrounding mental-ill-health and suicide. A need to give people an alternative. Bronwen's vision was for every person to have access to effective suicide prevention that is informed or led by people with lived experience.

Roses in the Ocean was born.

At its heart are people with lived experience of suicide. Their purpose is to save lives and reduce the emotional distress and pain of others. They are dedicated to empowering others to find their voice, and to bring their insights and wisdom to suicide prevention by raising suicide awareness and supporting survivors, their loved ones, and those left behind when someone dies by suicide.

Roses in the Ocean seeks to lead the significant cultural shift needed to save lives by harnessing the perspectives of all they represent, along with their own lived experience of suicide. This has led to opportunities to influence system reform.

Roses in the Ocean foregrounds the importance of hearing the voices of those with lived experience. The knowledge they share is inspiring; no two people's narratives are the same. Education about suicide and advocating for those that have attempted or died by suicide is so needed. By sharing real-life stories, Roses in the Ocean educates those of us who have not been down this path.

Each voice inspires, supports, heals, and holds space.

Chapter 33
Continuing and Ongoing Care

Every person on your loved one's medical team – including you – wants a successful transition to living outside a hospital setting.

— Sarah

The best place to practice continuing care is while our loved ones are in the hospital. All the decisions in the unit are made in conjunction with doctors, nurses, and the allied health team, with the collaboration of your loved one and their nominated carer. Once they are discharged, the person who is taking care of them takes on more responsibilities.

I'm going to sneak in a bit of information about long term care in hospitals. If your loved one is admitted to hospital, they may be there for days, weeks, months or longer. If you are paying for hospital parking, please speak with the parking attendant at the carpark checkout, or your social worker or nurse in charge of the unit, to see if parking is subsidised. Many hospitals offer this, but sadly it is not advertised.

When our loved ones are in hospital for any length of time it can have far-reaching effects. Work-life balance is important, especially if you have suddenly become the sole income earner. If your loved one needs time off work, is that taken as a leave of absence or sick leave? Are you able to discuss this with your loved one? If not, speak to your medical team to see if they have suggestions, as they may be able to tell you the right words to explain their absence from work.

What can we bring into the ward?

Are pets allowed in the unit for a visit? Or self-soothing items our loved one may need?

Spending hours each day visiting someone in hospital can lead to boredom. So, what can you do there? Start a hobby, write a book (not as far-fetched as it sounds), poetry, knitting, crosswords.

The ward will have specific visiting hours so every patient can rest, have tests done and attend events such as music and art therapy, sessions with their psychiatrist and psychologist.

Your loved one is in a safe space and place. Reassess how much time you need to spend at the hospital. It's ok to spend time away.

Other concerns to think about

- Expenses of getting to and from hospital. Bring lunch or a snack with you.
- Self care often gets forgotten. Check in with yourself and others in the household or others that share care with you.
- Allocate a certain amount of time each day for the three R's: Restore, Recharge and Revitalise.
- Are you working and has it been impacted?
- Do you need to speak with an accountant or financial adviser to ensure plans are put in place to have money to pay the bills.

Leave from the hospital

If your loved one is well enough, they may be able to take leave from the hospital. This may be for a special event or a just a change of scenery, for an hour or for a full day. Planning for these events ahead of time is important, without a doubt. It is a journey into the unknown, especially the first time. And navigating their return to hospital can be challenging. Make sure your loved one is happy to leave the security of the unit and feels that it is their choice. Remember, so much has been taken away from them – leave is a chance to give them back some agency. Let's put some plans in place.

Talk with your loved one as soon as you can after you find out they have leave.

- Do they want to go?
- What would *they* like to do?
- They may not have the capacity to decide. Give them two options catering to them, not you (sorry).

Walk through some scenarios with them and discuss their expectations and any boundaries that might help them (and you).

- If you have a pet, can they come with you?
- Are there places or things that are best avoided?
- Loud noises.
- Conflict with siblings or others.
- Over stimulation.
- Crowds.

Speak with staff and ask for suggestions on what to do and, importantly, on how best to return to the unit. If possible, have another family member or friend with you, as if things go south there are two of you to assist each other and your loved one.

When you are out on leave, look for visual and verbal cues from your loved one to assess how they are coping.

- Jiggling or shaking.
- Arguing, anger, or silence.

If things don't go as planned, ring the unit and speak with the nursing staff about what you can do to improve the situation. If you need to come back to the unit early, that's ok. Every step forward is positive. We brought our beautiful groodle with us in the car to pick our girl up and then walk her back to the entry door on her return. Before we left the unit, we discussed that she would be returning.

Leave is a positive step forward as it means your loved one's health is improving. Make sure your loved one knows that this is a significant step, and how proud of them you are. If your loved one can have leave and you feel comfortable going for a walk or drive to the local park for a picnic, I would suggest this as a first step.

The first time our girl was given a few hours leave was disastrous.

A reflection: continuing care sometimes means we go backwards, and that's okay.

On arrival at the ward one day, the nurses told me that my daughter had leave for a few hours. I leapt at the chance – lunch up the road would be brilliant. What could go wrong?

First mistake and rookie error. I didn't ask the nurses for any suggestions on where to go or what to do.

Second mistake. I *told* my girl that we were going up the road to sit and eat a burger.

I didn't ask, I told her.

Third mistake. The hospital is in the middle of the city. With that comes the hustle and bustle of crowds and loud noises, very loud noises and lots of them. A perfect recipe for overstimulation.

Fourth mistake. The moment we left the silence and safety of the ward, my daughter became agitated. I ignored it. I wanted us to be 'normal and boring', doing an activity, like any other mother and daughter going for lunch.

She was psychotic, hearing many voices in her brain, yet here I was dragging her out the door of her safe place to a cacophony of noise.

Fifth mistake. We kept going to the burger shop. We sat, I ordered, and my girl immediately wanted to leave. Everything was overwhelming her.

Sixth mistake. I finally realised my mistake, but I still made both of us sit and eat our burgers. I was desperate to make it happen. More for me than for her, I think. As soon as I realised this was not a great idea, I should have asked for takeaway or simply left. But I was determined to make this a positive experience for us both. It was not.

The positive? The only positive about this was leaving the burger place and walking back to the ward.

On returning, I made my girl a coffee, settled her in her room and went to speak to the nurses. They looked at me in horror as I recounted to them our awful hour. One of them said, 'oh! There's a beautiful little park five minutes walk away. It's secluded and very peaceful – you should have taken her there!'

Lesson learnt. When we went out on leave again a few days later, I was filled with anxiety but also a steely determination. I packed a bag of goodies, a thermos of tea, and we went to the park. There was no one else around. It was just us, until the rain came – but even that was fun.

Making mistakes can be horrible in the moment, but if we can gain knowledge from them, that's a positive. As time goes by as carers, it's easy to forget that we have become experts in looking after our loved one and helping them manage their complex mental health concerns. We have earnt those stripes, so we should wear them proudly. We already have knowledge of what has worked for our loved ones, and what hasn't.

Earlier I talked about putting each and every thing in your toolkit to pull out when needed. The thing is, not everything during recovery or continuing care is going to go perfectly. They may not even go well.

Stepbacks

Stepbacks is my word for removing ourselves from a situation, a time when something hasn't gone to plan, stepping back and looking with fresh eyes, or asking someone else to view the situation through their eyes. Others may call this reflective practice. Like my day taking my daughter to the burger place, I needed to stepback and look at myself with a critical eye. I'm glad I did.

When stepbacks happen, what actions can we do to get back on track?

> Firstly, speak with your loved one and ask if they have any suggestions.
> Always start with them, the solution may be looking straight back at you.
> Ask for help from your psychiatrist, psychologist and allied health team.
> Be specific about what the problem is.

If you are not getting an answer or a solution, remember the role of your social worker. Ask them for assistance and, importantly, that you would like the issue and its resolution documented in your loved one's medical notes for future reference.

There is a tremendous community of carers out in the world that can assist you. Utilise them. All you need is one suggestion to put in your toolkit, it may spark an idea or indeed a solution.

Allied health professionals come with a wealth of knowledge and experience. When our loved ones are well enough to leave hospital, they should leave with a care plan that is suitable for them. Remember, as your loved one's carer, you are a member of that team.

When there's mention of your loved one coming home, preparation is key

Every person on your loved one's medical team – including you – wants a successful transition to living outside a hospital setting. Speaking with your loved one and helping them manage their expectations is imperative. Start by asking:

What are their hopes and fears?
What are their expectations of you?
What boundaries will help support them?

If this is a matter of contention or robust discussion, ask your counsellor, social worker to help you navigate the negotiation. They are there to advocate and mediate for patients and carers – so what better time than now?

Once there's a whisper of discharge, ask to meet with the medical team, and organise a family meeting with you and your loved one involved. Ideally, this is where you will discuss a plan that suits everyone but focuses on your loved one. In the week prior to discharge, ask for a final team meeting to discuss any last queries or concerns.

Preparing you, your family and home for your loved one's discharge from hospital

Focus on you first. What do you need to put in order? Are you ok? Self care is necessary and needed. Do you have a support network of people that are there for you? Mental ill-health can be silent and I understand that it may be difficult to share with others. If this is the case, consider joining some forums, visiting carer websites. I'll mention Uniting, a not-for-profit organisation.

- Counselling or support groups for you.
- Respite care for YOU. Get your calendar out and book or schedule a break in now.
- YOU time: gym, golf, walk, lunch, haircut, coffee date ... anything that is for you.

Are you taking time off work to be with your loved one for a few days or longer? If so, organise and talk with your boss about the leave you are taking. What is expected of you if you are working from home. If working from home, is everything set up? Logins, computer, a working space?

What needs to be done to get your home ready?

I'll put some suggestions here but of course work out what's best for you and all those who live with you. Be mindful of changing anything in your loved one's room. Perhaps they can do it with you when they get home.

- Sharp implements locked up or hidden.
- Medications locked up or hidden.
- Do front and back doors need to be locked, so there is no wandering?
- Ongoing mental health appointments added to the calendar.

If there are things listed that you know are a concern, discuss them with the allied health team who have been involved with your loved one.

A specific area for your loved one to spend time in during the day. A little nook somewhere outside of their bedroom. Perhaps a hammock outside. Is this safe? Are there cords that could be a danger? If so remove. How about a bean bag? Create a quiet space just for them.

Family members should be aware of what to do or who to call in an emergency. All numbers should be clearly visible.

- PECC unit
- National emergency number
- Psychiatrist
- Psychologist
- Mental health outpatient department
- Next-of-kin mobile numbers
- Trusted friend

If possible, have a discussion with those living with you about expectations and concerns they may have. What are your boundaries or no-go zones? Do they need to be discussed with your loved one while they are still in hospital? If you would like support during this talk, ask your social worker or nurse.

Boundaries or no-go zones.

- Limited TV time
- Times for mobile phone usage
- Gaming time, or screen time
- Behaviours you will ignore and others you won't
- Your stance on drugs and alcohol.

Make a list of goals or plans. These are malleable and can be implemented at any time. Go through them with your loved one. Be aware that your loved one may not have the capacity or desire to talk about any sort of plan. Discuss goals that are achievable in the now with your loved one and their mental health team. Will you have a schedule or plan for each day organised? It may be as simple as the time to get out of bed/shower/breakfast/activity.

One task to achieve that day might be one of these:

- Get out of bed.
- Get out of pyjamas.
- Walk the dog.
- Draw in an adult colouring book.
- Speak to their psychiatrist, psychologist, or counsellor.
- Keep that appointment.
- Put a load of washing on.
- Responsibility for loading or unloading the dishwasher or washing or drying the dishes.
- One smile or hug a day.

Every step forward, no matter how tiny, is a positive. Even stepbacks are ok because we can learn from them. Every bit of information we learn goes into that toolkit so we can be armed with the positives and the negatives. Soon you'll be adding more things that are continually successful than the negatives.

Go you!

Build your own toolkit - some examples

What is negotiable and non-negotiable to maintain emotional safety?

- Boundaries regarding marijuana or other illicit drugs / alcohol in the home.
- Gaming and screen time usage restricted to a certain number of hours per day but negotiable.
- Personal space and self-care.
- Medical appointments
- Sensitivities or things that cause strong emotional reactions, such as friendships and relationships that are negative.

Chapter 34
Self Care

As carers, we often forget about ourselves, our concerns and our needs.

— Sarah

As carers, we can live with sadness, guilt, loneliness, silence, fatigue, stress, and a multitude of 'if only's'. You may be thinking, who's going to help me with everything that needs to get done? This may involve picking up the kids from school or activities, paying the bills, further studies, organising appointments and more. These might be tasks your loved one usually does or helps with and can't at the moment, or they might need to be redistributed according to your family's new roles (see chapter on Early Care). Looking after yourself can get lost among all these changes. Many of us carry emotional sadness and more, but it's how we deal with it that matters.

I know what it's like to sit in the car in the driveway after finishing a shift at work. Sitting for seconds, minutes, and hours before I could get out. I'd set my smile in place, not knowing what tentacle of mental health would be waiting for me when I eventually walked through the front door.

It can be draining to hold space for our loved one when they are at their lowest, to absorb their verbal grenades and dodge the vitriol that comes from their mouth, and to listen to the deafening silence if they will no longer talk or are no longer with us. We wait for the positive moments and celebrate them, and remember that tomorrow will bring a new day. Perhaps a brief smile. A nod. A hug. The briefest glimmer of hope keeps us going.

What about you?

It is important that we look after ourselves. Burnout in carers is real.

- Book that appointment with a counsellor, GP, psychologist, or psychiatrist.
- Have a valued friend or a fellow carer to listen to *you*.
- Write your thoughts down in a diary or a journal.
- Call a helpline, or join in on a carers' forum or discussion.
- Book regular respite care for your loved one so you can step away to recharge. This can give you and your loved one a well-needed break from each other, in the nicest possible way.
- Carer groups, forums, and groups on social media can give us a space to be heard without judgement, and can offer education and a different perspective.
- In-person support groups, such as mens' sheds, can be found through community centres or your local council.
- Practicing gratitude – for those who help bring our loved ones home or keep them safe, or for any small step forward – can help us focus on the positive.
- Self-care looks different to everyone, but ultimately it is *you* time. It might involve beautification, meditation,

exercise, reading, visiting a cafe or library, going to a concert or play, or even returning to work.
- Try to see friends, especially if you haven't for a while.

As carers, we often forget about ourselves, our concerns, and our needs. Money is often spent on our loved one's care, leaving little for our needs. But looking after ourselves doesn't have to be expensive. Universities, TAFEs, and training centres may offer free or heavily discounted treatments and services, from hair and beauty to restaurants to tax clinics. There is a catch, of course; these are delivered by students who are still learning. But if they have no one to practice on, then how can they become the next best thing?

One of the amazing things I found is the Australian College of Applied Psychology (ACAP). They offer free psychology, social work, and counselling services via Zoom or face to face, in Sydney, Melbourne, Adelaide and Perth.

Self care also involves navigating the stigma and silence of mental ill-health

Psychologist Dr Amanda Ferguson interviewed a friend of mine, Michelle Scheibner, on her podcast *Psych for Life*. Michelle had written a book called *Hush: a memoir unravelling the unintended legacy of family secrets*. On the podcast they discussed caring for a loved one who has passed away, and the grief, loss, love, and confusion it left behind. This hit home, and I realised how much sadness I had kept inside myself.

My darling daughter had suggested for years that I speak with a professional, whether it be a counsellor or psychologist. I automatically said no. I mean, what would I have to say to them? It took me nine years to see a psychologist. There is no doubt I have trauma borne from those first few years entangled in the tentacles of mental ill-health. It was too hard to shake them off, and surprisingly easy to live with them, slowly wrapping themselves around me.

Dear Carer,

When you are ready, you will speak, and you will be heard. It doesn't matter whether it's a counsellor, a helpline, a friend or fellow carers. You don't need to do this alone. Sometimes we need to hear the words from others to start making a change. Dr Amanda Ferguson, has some wise words for carers:

> 'Keep looking after yourself while looking after your loved ones, so that you can continue to do so. Seek personal support, guidelines, support groups and professional help if needed. Know your thresholds and situational boundaries and what actions to take and to not take in potential scenarios. Especially know when, where and how to 'hand over' your loved one.
>
> I have found *Spiritual Emergency*, a book by psychiatrist Stanislav Grof, helpful. Despite being about psychological change, any major life crisis requires an expanded questioning of suffering and meaning if we are to fully heal'.
>
> — Dr Amanda

Unsolicited advice

An important part of self-care is guarding against well-meaning people who give unsolicited advice. What to say to others who offer (not always) well-meaning advice.

- I'd prefer not to get advice on this right now. I just need you to listen.
- I understand you want to help, but this isn't something I need advice on.
- I hear you, but I'm comfortable with the approach we are taking.
- That's an interesting approach but I'm not looking for advice at the moment.

- It's not easy for me to speak about mental ill-health and my loved one. I'd appreciate if you could listen without judgement.
- I appreciate your perspective, but we have plans and practices in place.
- Thank you, but I have a toolkit of advice and suggestions that are tried and tested for us.

If these don't work, sometimes a straightforward approach is necessary.

- It seems you have a lot of knowledge of this subject. I'm wondering where you heard that? (This may actually encourage the person to share their lived experience).
- Let me stop you there. I don't appreciate what you are saying. I respectfully ask that you stop.
- I understand you are coming from what you think is a good place, but you need to stop. Quite frankly, what you are saying is offensive.
- I'd like to suggest that you enrol in a mental health first aid course. You can find them online. I know you'd find it helpful and educational.
- This is none of your business.

And if these don't work? Walk away.

Those living with mental health concerns don't have bandages, sutures, or plaster to show for it. But there is stigma and often silence that follows them every day. By association, these can follow carers too. Seeking out spaces to share, listening and being heard is part of ensuring we maintain our own mental health while our loved one recovers.

I've always tried to think outside the box for self care. I would never have thought of volunteering as self care, but of course it is. Seeing the joy on others faces when they receive kindness – no matter in what form – is inspiring.

Self care can come under the guise of volunteering

I have a wonderful nurse colleague who volunteers and assists homeless people. She cleans wounds, changes dressings or bandages, and chats to those she treats. Other volunteers prepare meals and drinks from the food van, which sometimes brings washing machines and dryers, and a selection of new or donated clothes to choose. I have another friend who volunteers at an inner-city shelter for animals or as our family says, fur babies. Some more options are at the local library, men's sheds, animal shelters, meals on wheels.

Ultimately it comes down to what you love doing. Volunteering is not for everyone but a suggestion to add for another day.

What being silent taught me and how it helped me with my own self care

One thing I wouldn't have changed is the silence we, as a family, kept in the first years of our mental health expedition. We advocated for our daughter in and out of hospital and to medical personnel, but when it came to speaking to anyone else, we did not share.

Why wouldn't I change this? Because our loved one was not ready, and we weren't either. I just couldn't say the words or express the grief we were going through out loud. Mostly I think I was scared to see the judgment or feel the stigma from others.

If no one knew, nobody would judge us or whisper behind our backs. There was a price to pay for hiding our ever-so-secret secret. It was draining, and my social and work batteries were continually on charge mode.

Why did I change my mind?

Breaking that silence was one of the hardest things I have done. As a family, we discussed the positives and the negatives. It had to be at the right time, and we were of the feeling that it was one in, all in. Our main focus was our daughter, if she was yes for talking about mental ill-health then we would be too. For us, sharing our story has been cathartic. I think perhaps it pointed us all in directions we never would have gone in otherwise. Our focus has become breaking that silence for those that cannot or do not want to.

Complex mental health has taught me to accept the sadness, grief and loss but to express those feelings, so they don't consume me. On the other side it has shown me compassion, love and strength that I never knew I had. Don't let those tentacles of mental health pull you down, and if they do, ask for help. Reach out to a trusted friend, colleague or helpline.

> *One of my main tips for carers, I would say, is self-care. I always use the plane analogy – you put your own oxygen mask on before you can help others. Carer burnout is real. I take my hat off to carers as it's often a long, exhausting road.*
>
> — Trish

Chapter 35
Friend Care

The real work needs to be done with the general population: friends, health-care workers (yes, especially this group), schools and other educational facilities.

— Sarah

As carers, it's often difficult to put into words what we are living through. As a friend, family member, or colleague of someone who is living with, or caring for someone with, complex mental health conditions, it is often hard to know what to do or what to say. This chapter is for friends, allies, and supporters, and for carers to share with others.

Friends and supporters

The band of people who will support and listen without judgement are allies. Complex mental health concerns are a chronic illness, just like diabetes or heart, kidney, or lung disease. There is often a deafening silence that goes with complex mental health concerns, even from friends and allies. This is often a shock to carers who struggle to ask for help; stigma rears its head yet again. Sharing what is happening behind closed doors may be emotionally hard. How others react and what words come out of their mouths can, sadly, be insensitive, to say the least.

If a colleague is diabetic and has a hypo (low blood sugar episode) at work, we don't blink an eye about learning what we can do to assist. If someone has an anxiety or depressive episode, it is often met with silence and confusion. No one knows what to do or say. This needs to change.

Five simple steps to show support

1. Ask the person how they're doing.
2. Listen.
3. Don't judge.
4. Ask what *you* can do. Don't tell them what you think they need to do.
5. Don't share about their life without their consent. It isn't yours to tell. In other words, don't gossip.

There is still much to do to change the narrative of complex mental health. We can start through education. Here is a brief story as to why.

Nurses are required to earn continuing professional development (CPD) points every year that we work. These are specific to what field we work in. For me, it is in operating theatres, admission, recovery, anaesthetics, and discharge. We call this the perioperative unit. I work with the most amazing and wonderful team and have been working at the same hospital for over fifteen years.

Why am I telling you this?

Because we do not receive mandatory mental health first aid training. As nurses, we receive mandatory basic life support (BLS) and advanced life support training (ALS). We receive this training as it is expected that if a medical emergency happens that we will know what to do. It is our duty of care. Likewise, we receive manual handling training, so we can learn what to move and lift without injury, and fire training, so we know what to do in any particular fire event.

Mental health training is *not* mandatory for nursing staff. This is why we need to change the narrative for all no matter where we work, live or go to school. Mental health first aid training is needed. If you have not enrolled in a course, then why not do it today? Education is key to awareness and knowledge of what to do and how. The real work needs to be done with the general population: friends, health-care workers (yes, especially this group), schools and other educational facilities.

I once spoke to a senior nurse at another hospital and suggested that they send their staff on a mental health first aid training and a suicide prevention course. I was astounded at the reply. They looked me straight in the eyes, laughed and said, 'If I do that, and someone comes to see me with concerns, then I'll have to do something about it.'

Then and there I knew I needed to change the narrative, and you, my dear friends, can help.

How can you learn more about complex mental health?

Do the mental health first aid course. Organise those with lived experience of mental ill-health to speak at your workplace, school, or university. SANE Australia, the Black Dog Institute and Beyond Blue offer these services and many more.

What to do for a friend who is an inpatient at a psychiatric unit?

- Ask if you can visit. Check the unit's website or ask staff what you can and can't bring them, and what the process is for entering the ward (you may be asked to place items like belts, shoelaces, mobile phone in a locker while you visit)
- Ask your friend what they would like to do when you visit.
- You might play an instrument, listen to music or a podcast, or join them in a ward activity, like yoga, Pilates, or art.
- Depending on how tired their brain is, they may not be able to concentrate on things for very long. This means they might struggle to read, write, draw or watch television. This equates to BOREDOM. If you bring a book or a magazine to leave with them, you may be able to read to them. The next person coming to visit can take over from where you left off.
- Bring a home-cooked meal, coffee or a milkshake ... we all know how hospital food is! Make sure you clear it with the nursing staff first to avoid allergies, food intolerances or interaction with medications.

Remember, all they may want or need is for you to hold space with them. Shhhh! This means silence. Don't give up on them if they don't want you to visit. There are other ways to stay in contact. Persistence may become your middle name.

What can you do for your friend who is a carer?

The same as you would for any friend!

- If they are ready to talk to you about mental health, ask them questions and let them know that you are there for them.
- They may want to forget the caring side of life and just be away from home or hospital for a few hours.
- Go for a walk or a swim with them if that's their thing.
- Breakfast, lunch or dinner date.
- Gift them a massage, beauty therapy, or two tickets to a concert, the movies or a sporting event.
- Just be with them and hold space.
- Ask, 'what can I do for you?'
- Most importantly, listen and do not judge. This is their life. Let them talk.
- If their mental health is at risk or they are in an unsafe situation, tell somebody, Call 000 if you need to.
- If you are unsure how they really are, ask them. Say the words: Are you ok? Are you thinking of hurting yourself? Are you thinking of suicide?

Act on what they tell you, guiding, not judging. Suggest an appointment with their local doctor. Offer to help arrange a counselling appointment. Contact emergency services if required.

Friends need self care too. Check in with yourself and remember the three R's: Restore. Recharge. Revitalise.

Chapter 36
Legal Care

A power of attorney can be made only if the person has the mental capacity to understand the document and what they are signing.

— Senior Counsel James

A few formalities before I start this chapter. This chapter does not constitute legal advice – please seek guidance from those who practice law in your state or country if you need legal assistance.

Remember, mental health legislation does not fall under one umbrella. Each country (and each state in Australia) has its own legislation. It can be helpful to know your rights and your health care providers' responsibilities in your local area.

I have spoken with a lawyer, Senior Counsel James, who practices in the state of New South Wales in Australia, for this chapter on legal care. But, in all honesty I could not write about the law without consulting my very learned ninety-five-year-old father, a King's Counsel, former Deputy Senior Crown Prosecutor and retired District Court Judge. It will make Papa happy to be acknowledged, as he's still as sharp as a tack and as knowledgeable as ever. Papa perused these words with sharp eyes but not an argument or debate was to be found with our Senior Counsel.

I encourage you to develop a plan to ensure the future needs of you, your family and your loved ones are met prior to a medical emergency happening.

Chapter 37
Wills, power of attorney and enduring guardians

I spoke to Senior Counsel James, who practises in New South Wales, Australia, and has many years of experience in law specialising in wills, trusts and probate.

James, can you tell us about wills?

A valid will is made by somebody over the age of eighteen with testamentary capacity. Testamentary capacity is a legal test and not a medical test, although we take on board the guidance of a medical practitioner who might indicate that somebody was suffering from Alzheimer's disease or dementia, or delirium, at or about the time they made the will. Unless there are exceptional circumstances, you have to be over eighteen to make a will.

A will remains valid even if the person loses testamentary capacity. It can be changed to suit individual circumstances that have changed; for example, marriages and partnerships end, children grow up and other life happenings occur.

If you give a benefit to somebody under a will and they're over eighteen, they usually get the immediate benefit of it. Whether it's a lump sum, real estate, or an annuity or life interest.

If you are concerned about how a benefit under a will might be dealt with (for example, if a beneficiary cannot handle finances), your executor can seek to have a financial manager appointed for the beneficiary.

You can sometimes leave money to somebody in trust. In other words, a trustee controls the administration of the money. It's appropriate to seek legal guidance on this.

How can we ensure our loved one's bills are paid?

This is where you need to be mindful of the executor. An executor is a trustee, company or individual appointed in a will to administer the deceased's estate. The role includes legal and financial responsibilities that can be time consuming and complicated. The executor is empowered to pay the bills, but there has to be a fund established for this. If you have an asset, you need the capital to maintain it.

If someone has a psychiatric condition or dementia, or a significant medical event has occurred, you can separate the right to live in the property from the financial side, but you need to create a fund to maintain it.

James, can you tell us what a power of attorney is?

It's a legal document where one person (the 'principal' – in this case, our loved one) gives another person or persons (the 'attorney' or 'joint attorneys') authority to make legal and financial decisions on their behalf.

Powers of attorney are important for overseeing someone's affairs during travel or where the principal is not otherwise available. Powers of attorney can have a broad lens covering financial, legal and property matters. A power of attorney can be made only if the principal has the mental capacity to understand it.

Be careful in choosing your attorney – they must be trustworthy, as they may be making financial and legal decisions on your behalf or on behalf of your loved one.

Powers of attorney can be revoked at any time. For example, if a power of attorney commenced because of psychosis or diminished or no mental capacity, then on recovery, the power of attorney can cease.

My advice is to seek legal advice for further clarity.

What is an enduring guardian?

This is a trusted person appointed by you to make health and lifestyle decisions on your behalf. For example, I appoint you my enduring guardian like a power of attorney, but only to operate when a doctor (this can be stated as a specific specialty, such as psychiatry) certifies that I'm not capable of giving rational instructions at this time.

An enduring guardian sounds the same as a power of attorney.

Enduring guardianship appoints someone to make personal, health and lifestyle decisions if they lose mental capacity. This needs to be put in place when our loved one is in positive mental health.

- Power of attorney is appointed for financial and legal matters.
- The guardian and attorney can be the same person or someone else.
- Seeking legal advice while our loved ones are in good health is the aim.
- Ask your legal counsel for the nuances of both.

In some states of Australia, people know a guardian as a substitute decision maker.

There is a tribunal that can review the power of attorney and guardianship yearly, or more often if required, to ensure that it is working as it should be or if there is a conflict of interest.

Can we complete this form ourselves or is it advisable to get these documents to be noted by a lawyer?

It is best to be done in consultation with a lawyer. In some cases, the law requires the documents to include certain information. Your lawyer will advise you of the most appropriate and up-to-date information and legal terminology.

From our trauma-informed clinician Aliceson.

As carers, advocacy is at the heart of all that we do for our loved ones. Aliceson, what does it look like in your role when someone has or has not formalised guardianship arrangements?

If your loved one is under an Australian mental health act and you are the designated and documented carer, someone will keep you informed about your loved one's care, and you should be included in any meetings.

If your loved one is not under a mental health act, the sharing of information is guided by their consent. It is good practice for services to keep checking in with the consumer (your loved one) about this and not assume that this doesn't change. Even if the consumer does not consent to the sharing of information, services can still support and listen to families and carers.

It poses a challenging situation for families and carers when a loved one refuses to give consent for them to receive information, causing significant distress. It is good practice for clinicians to be engaged with families and carers. There may not be consent to share information, but that does not stop families or carers from providing information and for clinicians to be gathering this information as a part of building their understanding of the consumer and the surrounding system.

Chapter 38
Financial Care

Get your financial house in order.

— Jacqui

This will be a brief chapter, as the best advice is to speak to a financial adviser or accountant to understand the most suitable options for you. Or check out the financial section in your local library for ideas you can put into action.

My experience floundering over money

When mental ill-health arrived in our family, so did unexpected medical bills that sent us into a spin. I had taken leave from work to care for our girl, and things started to build up. We paid the bills but there was nothing left over. The mortgage was an incredible weight on top of medical bills. Financially, I felt like we were drowning.

Our girl knew the financial cost of speaking with a psychiatrist, and we knew she would stop going if the financial burden was too much for us. She questioned us on a number of occasions if we were ok for her to keep seeing her psychiatrist. For us, at this time, these appointments were non-negotiable. If we could do it, we would. This was a positive for us. Because, let's face it, we need to find the wins or else we'd cry. And the best-case scenario was to keep her out of hospital, and psychiatrist appointments helped us do that.

I am well aware that having a roof over our head is a blessing. That there are many struggling paying the rent or mortgage and putting food on the table. This is when we need to reach out to those who help care for the carers. Utilise government resources, not-for-profit foundations and institutes that are there for us. Find someone who can assist you in the minefield of healthcare and make sure you and your loved ones are receiving your rightful benefits from the government.

Build your own toolkit

- Superannuation
- Income Protection
- Legalities
- Financial adviser
- When are the bills and/or rent due? Put in calendar.
- If you have a mortgage or other debt, how much is owed and when are repayments due?
- Speak to an accountant.
- Keep track of incoming invoices and payments.
- Start a spreadsheet and reminder on phone.
- Do you require a weekly or monthly budget?
- Separate bank accounts. One with everyday spending money and the other with savings.
- Bank accounts that need both your and your partner's passwords to remove money from the account.

Chapter 39
Jacqui's story: stop worrying about your money

I spoke with Jacqui Clarke, a trusted adviser, board member, executor, veteran business executive, and author. She has worked with families for decades to help them preserve, protect and grow their wealth and, most importantly, to navigate the challenges that money brings.

Jacqui has written a book called *Stop worrying about your money*. In the book, she talks about getting your financial house in order by dealing with worry and planning for the future. She covers all the financial topics we need to be aware of when caring for someone with health concerns.

Jacqui, how do I make sure my loved one doesn't spend the money or lose the house I am leaving them in my will?

Establish a protective trust – this will enable someone else you trust to be a guardian over the money for this family member, and you can allow income rather than capital to be provided to them. You can design a protective trust for specific needs. For example, you might have enough money for a house, but you need to allow for upkeep and rates. Add these questions to those you will ask your legal representative.

At a minimum, what should we have in place for our loved one financially?

Ensure that all assets are protected. Make sure that decision making is shared so that things don't happen without your knowledge – such as money being used for unnecessary items or misuse of funds. You need to have your own financial house in order.

Understand whose name is on the title of things, especially your house or investment property. Make sure you continue to focus on your super. I always recommend that couples share bank accounts, but sometimes separate finances are necessary.

You have to be vigilant – as I say in my book, 'know what it costs to open your front door' so you will immediately see if there are any leakages from your savings. When someone is unable to make decisions, ensure a power of attorney has been established. Having formal documentation at your fingertips when a crisis happens, especially if there are siblings, children, or others that live under your roof, can only be a positive.

Chapter 40
Personal stories of lived experience

Each story is powerful, and every word beats with the heart and passion of the carer and those they love and advocate for. Every. Single. Day.

— Sarah

When I started writing *Dear Carer,* I pondered for a while between the use of the words 'story' and 'journey'. In my mind, a journey has a beginning and an end, a start and a finish. Do complex mental health conditions have an end? Is there a conclusion? Complex mental health, to me, will always have a comma after it. A story is ongoing ... so, I threw *journey* out and have kept *story* in.

Woven through the pages of this book are stories where carers have recounted their truth. They have shared their emotions and innermost thoughts. Each story is powerful, and every word beats with the heart and passion of the carer and those they love and advocate for. Every. Single. Day.

The stories are from Australia and the USA. I really wanted to show that no matter where we live in the world, mental health lives too. I wish I could have included more lived experiences from around the world; I am certainly open to hearing them. Carers loving, living with, and looking after those with complex mental health conditions are in a tricky place. Most will not talk about it; if they do, it is under strict instruction that the person they are talking to will not share.

When carers find another carer, it is a most wonderful thing. Long-held secrets are shared, sometimes spoken out loud for the first time. Fears, guilt, grief, exhaustion, vulnerability, and hope for the future are talked about openly and honestly.

We feel heard.
We feel seen.
We do not feel judged.

Our stories are not the same, which makes each individual experience special. Sometimes we need to listen to others' stories to understand our own better. If we can take away one solitary idea, and it becomes a positive step forward in our loved one's recovery – or our own – then it is worthwhile. Feeling understood through shared vulnerability is equally important. At other times, we need a way to share our grief, our sadness, our despair over the path our loved one's life has taken. And let's be honest, over losing the life we thought we'd be leading as we got older.

Why us, why you, why me?

We are parents, sibling, nurses, doctors, electricians, personal assistants, lawyers, artists, cleaners, teachers, carers, shop assistants, students, counsellors, psychiatrists, psychologists, builders, chefs, politicians, writers, journalists, gardeners ... the list is ongoing.

We are just like you. Mental ill-health does not discriminate; it can cast a shadow of darkness and a cloak of stigma over any one of us.

The stories in this book are shared with a great deal of vulnerability, heart, strength, and compassion, with a smidge of anger and disappointment. At the centre of each is the advocacy that carers wear proudly. Each carer carries a sadness that more cannot be done, each has borne the feeling of being unseen and unheard.

Perhaps within these words you will see a touch of yourself or someone you know.

Lived experience: stories from the heart

After delivering a talk at a public hospital, a group of clinicians asked me if I'd be interested in speaking to groups of health care workers whose jobs *don't* centre on mental health.

Of course, I said yes. When I talk to groups in the complex mental health space, I'm preaching to the converted. When I said this to the clinicians, they nodded. One shared that they'd been called to a general surgical ward to discuss a patient who required a few nights in the hospital following their procedure. Upon the clinician's arrival at the ward, a nurse approached them and asked when they would move the patient to 'where they belong'.

The clinician was confused and astounded. This admission was for a surgical procedure, not for their mental health condition. The nurse stated that 'these people should be on their own mental health ward.' The clinician managed to contain their disappointment and disbelief, explaining that the patient was on the correct ward for the required treatment.

We need to do better.
We need to change the narrative.

Chapter 41
Cam and Charlie's story: living with ADHD, OCD, and diabetes

Country Victoria, Australia

We have all the knowledge and connections in the world and still have been unable to access treatment to keep our child safe.

— Cam

Cam is a mum I met through an online course on health and wellness. Like me, she has worked in the hospital system for a number of years. We bonded on a number of fronts including our shared experience of caring for a loved one with complex mental health concerns. Charlie is Cam's son, and lives with several medical diagnoses that make accessing medical care challenging. Charlie is a proud trans man living with diabetes, attention deficit hyperactivity disorder (ADHD) and obsessive-compulsive disorder (OCD).

Being unseen and unheard goes to the core of what our loved ones and their amazing carers live through, often on a daily basis and surprisingly in the places we least expect it - in a medical setting. The more stories we hear about complex health, the better we can understand and the more we can see people as who they are, not the diagnosis they have been labelled with.

Cam, can you tell us about your experience seeking healthcare?

My son Charlie is twenty-three years old and the oldest of my three kids. The most striking feature about him is his towering intellect. He is articulate and knowledgeable. He advocates for and speaks on behalf of his community, and people recognise his ability to create a safe space for those in need.

He is also a complex human being.

Last year, he battled for three months against suicidal thoughts. We tried everything we knew to access help, as it was beyond us to manage it alone. I'm a health professional, so I thought at least I knew who to ask. I thought no health crisis would demand a more urgent system response. I was wrong.

Instead, I've seen eyes averted and our case handballed around to every conceivable service. It feels as though Charlie's cries for help will only be heard when the worst has happened. I've tried to explain how impossible it has been to get help, but these days I'm stunned and silenced by it. Over the years, I've learned that when things are truly terrible, it's impossible to find help.

It's terrifying.

Cam, are you able to share a timeline of medical events?

Charlie was diagnosed with Type 1 diabetes at twenty-two months old. In the years since that time – and closely related to the ongoing experience of diabetes management – he has suffered from anxiety and depression. At sixteen he came out as transgender and has been a proud trans man ever since. At twenty-one, he was diagnosed with

ADHD. Charlie is likely somewhere on the autism spectrum and now has a diagnosis of OCD. Each of these facets of him has had a different and separate service response from the health industry. He has lived with a chronic illness for at least twenty years. And, from early primary school, mental ill-health joined in – although I didn't understand at the time that's what was happening.

How have you found accessing medical services?

Each service has been incredibly difficult to access. None of them have communicated with each other. Each has considered him from within their own specialist silo. None has seen Charlie as a whole person.

I can't separate what is happening now in a mental health context from what has happened over the years across other health services Charlie has needed to utilise. There is no community- or sector-wide approach to care that is preventative, it is all reactive and acute. What I know is that every single service we have tried to access has pushed us back to try somewhere else.

I'm told, 'It's lucky you're home to look after him'. It's not lucky. It doesn't feel lucky to have all the knowledge and all the responsibility and risk. We are asked, 'what do you want us to do?' We don't know. If we did, we would have told you. If we did, we probably wouldn't be here. I am told, 'Charlie is an adult, so we can't speak to you.' This is unacceptable, if not unethical; Charlie has given consent for me to speak for him. He has been so sick that he couldn't speak for himself. Not letting me speak for him effectively denies his care.

Mental health services do not consider Charlie's diabetes and its contribution to and interaction with his wellbeing and safety. Each specialist has told us, 'I am only able to help you with diabetes, or gender identity, or ADHD. I am not a crisis service.' Charlie is not just one of those diagnoses. He is a human being like the rest of us – made up of all those labels and plenty more. The silos of care have worked together to deny us access to care.

Nearly all services consider the fact that Charlie is transgender as the first issue for consideration, ignoring what he is actually saying to them about what is ailing him. Each service has said, 'If you're worried, go to the emergency department or call an ambulance.' It's a cop out, a handball, that sends us to the services that have consistently pushed us back.

Charlie has had to tell his story, the tale that triggers his anxiety, over and over again to the same services and, often, the same people.

We've had periods where Charlie's diabetes was brittle and difficult. In those times we were in contact with the diabetes educators who, when it got too close to call, advised us we should present to the emergency department for an infusion. Here they made us wait for hours and then turned us away, decreeing us – the knowledgeable parents – to be the 'best to care for Charlie'. I've always been too stunned and exhausted to speak louder in that moment; to tell them that's why we've come for help, because we are the 'carers who know him best'. And we recognise that he needs medical attention now.

Our health system needs to do better.

When I try to summarise this situation, I find I am unable to separate our experiences into the usual silos of the health system. Right now, mental health care is most urgent, but we have been pushed away when presenting for diabetes care as well. Again, none of our specialist services communicate with one another, and so no-one knows Charlie as a whole person. No one has considered him as a member of a family; a son, a nephew, a friend.

We have all the knowledge and connections in the world and still have been unable to access treatment to keep our child safe. The skills and knowledge we have has served only to keep us alone in this cycle longer, rather than supporting us to keep him well.

Charlie has had so many experiences of being told 'we can't help you' that he asked me if he is a hopeless case and should give up. I refuse to let this continue for the years to come. We deserve better ... other families deserve better.

I will always advocate for Charlie but these days, when others ask how he is, I often say nothing or, 'He's doing well.' It's easier than trying to explain again or having to respond to perceived judgement of the fact that he's not working and still lives at home, unlike others of his age. It's too hard and rarely understood.

Charlie is always going to live life hard. He has never given up and we will never either. For the first time in over twenty years, he has a competent, professional psychologist who seems to be committed to working with him through the complexity of his issues.

It's not wise to be hopeful, but I am.

Cam, has it taken a toll on you?

Constantly. Our families don't really understand, or find it distasteful, or would prefer not to have to deal with it. My sister, who deals with a similar issue, is a safe place to go. There's no misplaced judgement or advice from her, as it's someone who actually knows! I'm an open book until we skirt close to this one. Not sharing is a protective response.

Have you read any helpful books, received any helpful information, or found something that has worked for your family that you would recommend?

Hmm, I learn my most meaningful lessons in reading fiction. I love stories that depict someone wholeheartedly accepting the difference in another with curiosity and compassion.

What would you tell your younger self now?

That fear can fool you by masquerading as confidence. People don't offer help because they don't think I need it. There were opportunities for help when Charlie was at school that so terrified me. I mistook my strong instinct to run for wisdom, rather than for being scared. I was sometimes so frightened at the thought of telling someone, I didn't know what to do.

It's important I take care of myself. I walk. I write. I read. I catch up with my friends and try to enjoy life. All of it is separate to being a mum.

Chapter 42
Whitney and Skylar's story: living with Asperger's, OCD, schizophrenia, bipolar disorder, depression, and anxiety.

Victoria, Australia

> *Keep pushing the boundaries to get the proper help and medications needed, because no one else will advocate like you will for your loved one.*
>
> — Whitney

Whitney, can you share your story with complex mental health?

My daughter Skylar had intrusive thoughts and voices from the age of fourteen, but it was when she turned seventeen that things took a turn for the worse. Unbeknown to us, she had a plan to die by suicide. I am thankful Sky told someone. They listened and called the police. I don't think she thought they would do anything about it. My husband and I will be forever grateful that she was unsuccessful.

Dear Carer,

My daughter has been diagnosed with Asperger's, OCD, schizophrenia, bipolar disorder, depression, and anxiety. This is a lot to take in. To be honest, I cried. In fact, I still do. Skylar has had repeated hospitalisations because of suicidal thoughts, self-harm, that was cutting and burning herself.

Do your family and friends understand what complex mental health is?

Some of our relatives don't understand mental health concerns, let alone complex mental health conditions, and don't want to know anything about it or educate themselves. My mum sees Sky happy and immediately thinks her mental ill-health has gone away. I tell her that's not how it works. Sky has been in the public hospital system many times over the past fifteen years, in fact, when the voices first started.

Emergency rooms are notorious for waiting, have you had experience of this?

Emergency room waiting times are abysmal, especially when they are suicidal or psychotic. We spent hours waiting for a bed to become available and finally admitted. Our longest wait has been four days. Four days! Skylar visited the emergency department four times in one week, and they sent her home three of those times for self-harm and suicidal thoughts. She was finally admitted on her fourth presentation because someone listened to us. Before this, not one health care professional had heard us, that she needed to stay in hospital and could she please be seen by the psychiatric team.

As you can see, I have lost confidence in the health care system as it has failed us too many times.

What can hospital staff do better?

Skylar is not a statistic, a number, or a diagnosis.

I need acknowledgement from the medical staff of when and how they administer her medication. To confirm to me that she is in a safe environment. The trauma and lack of trust on my part are real. I need reassurance that Sky will not be mistreated by staff or other patients. And they will treat her with compassion. She is human and deserves dignity and respect. I would like health care workers to listen to the families that care for those with complex mental health. We have valuable information that needs to be shared.

There is stigma and fear in calling the police, and I am fortunate that I have not done this, but her friends have. The police have also escorted her to the hospital to keep her safe. I have then been called by the hospital informing us she is there. Sky doesn't want to 'hurt' me, and I don't mean in the physical sense. She says she doesn't want to cause me pain. She is the one in pain, and all I want to do is help her and make her safe.

How are you dealing with looking after you? Self care?

I am trying to advocate for my loved one, but my requests often fall on deaf ears. I live with guilt. The guilt of what we missed early in her life. Was there something I did wrong? Could I have done better? This led me to see a counsellor, and am getting support through talking with them. I run and go to the gym.

I also advocate for those with mental health concerns in the hospital and discuss with health care workers how we can improve. Prioritising communication with carers and the healthcare team is also a top priority for me.

Whitney, are you silent regarding Skylar's mental ill-health?

I am not silent about what diagnosis Skylar lives with. My family and mental health professionals need to know what help to give and understand her behaviour. My daughter is living in the now. She is a robotics engineer in the making, although studies are paused for the moment and we're unsure if her degree is on hold for now or the future.

You are doing an amazing job. How are you?

I cry a lot. Too much, for what could have been and what has gone on in the past and that our daughter has to live with. The self-harm, intrusive thoughts and what others think.

Our family dynamics have changed. My husband sees the positive. Whereas I live in fear for our daughter's safety and hope and pray that she stays alive and happy. My other kids say I treat Sky differently because of her mental ill-health. I don't mean to, but I live in constant fear and worry that I'll say something that stresses or touches on something sensitive for her, and she will end up in hospital again. It's like treading on eggshells all day, every day.

Today she is doing well. Not studying, but she is in a good place, and for that, we are happy.

Whitney, what advice do you have for others?

Keep advocating for your loved ones. Keep pushing the boundaries to get the proper help and medications needed because no one else will advocate like you will for your loved one. Write to your local and federal politicians, and tell them about your loved one's struggles. Make sure they include more mental health funding in future budgets.

What would you tell your younger self now that would help future you?

I would tell my younger self to look out for any signs of struggle or cries for help from my children. In saying that, I could see nothing out of the ordinary; this is probably because she hides her feelings from me, afraid of what will happen if I see her mental health decline.

Chapter 43
Helen and Emily's story: treatment-resistant depression, psychosis and bipolar disorder

North Carolina USA

> *I look to the positive, that Emily can function with us at home (cooking meals, laundry, etc) even if she is nowhere near as independent as she used to be.*
>
> — Helen

Helen, can you share how mental ill-health arrived in your family's lives?

This has been a hard journey, and we're still on it. I have a nursing background in cardiac care, but mental health is way above my level of understanding. My husband works in emergency medicine. I suspected we would have seen the signs, but our daughter Emily was living away at college, so we missed them all. Living with someone who has complex mental health is much different from treating someone in an acute care setting. This has become a completely different ballgame.

Our daughter started medical school in 2023 and moved away to college. She passed all her coursework but had sunk into depression. Doctors diagnosed Emily with treatment-resistant depression. They added more medications to the antidepressant she had started earlier that year. After much discussion, Emily decided the best option for her was to defer her studies for a year and focus on her health.

A year went by, and her depression had improved so much that, while my husband and I were on a trip to Alaska, Emily and her brother decided to go on a road trip to Massachusetts to see their cousins. We were on the ship approaching Alaska, living the dream, when we received a frantic call from our son telling us they'd arrived, but that Emily appeared to be psychotic, and had been admitted to the nearest hospital. Getting off the ship and onto a plane was filled with anxiety – every minute away from Emily was a minute not knowing what was happening.

When we arrived, information was hard to get – and we are medical people! It was frustrating and heartbreaking.

We live in North Carolina, and our hospital experience in Massachusetts, a twelve-hour drive away, wasn't great. We were relieved when the doctors released her into our care, allowing us to take her home. We are fortunate that we have medical insurance, access to a psychiatrist and the resources to care for her. Having both parents in the medical field has been a positive. When we brought her home to North Carolina, Emily was still unwell, but we were able to get her an EEG (electroencephalogram – a test that measures electrical activity in the brain. It can help diagnose other brain conditions that may be going on) and a head CT scan (these show a more detailed view of the tissue and blood vessels in your brain).

It was important for us to rule out any other diagnoses, and to ensure her medications were correct ... although that takes time.

Helen, have you ever had to call the emergency services?

In many states, including North Carolina, the sheriff transports psychiatric patients to inpatient facilities. That can be a shock. When Emily's psychosis occurred, an ambulance transported her to an inpatient facility. For this, we are indeed grateful.

What's your experience been like in the hospital system?

The American healthcare system can be a shitshow at the best of times. The best care costs money, and it should not be that way. I think Emily could have spent more time in the hospital. She was fortunate to be in a decent facility but would have benefitted from an intense hospital day-program. That said, we are beyond fortunate that she already had a psychiatrist.

Do you talk with others about mental ill-health?

For me, I have found talking to a friend and asking them for their perspective to be a wonderful sounding board. But I still struggle with talking about her mental health. Many of my friends are aware of my daughter's diagnosis. They are trusted friends and supportive. But Emily is not comfortable talking about her diagnosis, and since it is her story to tell, I have not told as many people as I otherwise would have.

I am an upfront person, and I feel that unless we stand up and talk about this illness, the stigma will never go away. But I have to consider her as well, so we remain silent. My friends and work colleagues who I have spoken with have been supportive. Some don't understand why she isn't working or back at school, but I don't think they realise the impact that mania, and especially the psychosis, has had on her cognitive ability. We feel it is important to let her brain recover and not add undue stress.

Can you share with us what you do for self care?

With the mental load we carry as carers, I'm grateful to keep moving, and I walk 5 to 6 kilometres a day. I meet with friends for lunch once a week, play mahjong a few times a month, work in my garden and go out to dinner with my husband. I also do some volunteer work with a few organisations in my area.

I look to the positive, that Emily can function with us at home (cooking meals, laundry, etc) even if she is nowhere near as independent as she used to be. We are hoping to get her into part-time work soon, but she sleeps quite a bit because of the medication she is taking. I have a wonderful husband and friends, but I feel very alone and out of control because I have no experience with complex mental health concerns such as bipolar. Emily is better, and we have the resources to cover her needs, but I worry about the future.

How are you?

I have guilt because I feel resentful of her at times. I don't want to be a caregiver. This time of life was supposed to be mine and my husband's. I know that sounds selfish, and she can't help it. My feelings are tough, and I muddle through them.

I have found a lot of helpful information through the National Alliance on Mental Illness (NAMI), the USA's largest mental health organisation. It's focused on those who live with complex mental health conditions and assisting them in making a difference. I am concerned about the future, especially government funding cuts for social security. If Medicaid gets cut, then heaven help most people with any type of disability.

Helen, can you share a tip or something that has surprised you?

It can be a lengthy process once your loved one is out of hospital for them to become stable. The first year after psychosis is so important for preventing a reoccurrence. Adjustments need to be made in caring for your loved one, no matter the age. I have had all the emotions: anger, grief, sadness, and guilt. I've also felt resentment for having to care for her. Saying these words to you, I feel horrible; I am glad Emily has never and will never know that I have had these emotions, but I want your readers to know that I have felt them. I've started therapy, which is incredibly helpful.

What would you tell your younger self that would help you now?

I would tell my younger self to research and read more. For almost ten years, my daughter had depression. I should have recognised this as a warning sign. A mood stabiliser medication may have prevented the mania and psychosis and treated her depression more successfully. I should have sought second opinions at academic medical centres. Finally, the importance of getting help or support for you, the caregiver.

Chapter 44
Maureen and Christopher's story: ADHD, bipolar and depression.

New Jersey, USA

> *I think mental ill-health hid beside or behind Christopher's ADHD diagnosis. If it were in plain sight, I didn't see it.*
>
> — Maureen

Maureen, can you share your mental health story, particularly when you first recognised it?

I'm a mother of four adult children. My husband died in 2007, so it has been me and the four kids, three of whom have varying degrees of mental health concerns. They're all adults now, but my youngest, Christopher, is the one I'll be talking about.

Christopher was diagnosed at eight years of age with ADHD, and was prescribed medication when he was in the third grade. He coped well, was an A-grade student and a happy kid. In sixth grade, Christopher told me he had trouble focusing. Then I noticed the decline in his grades; medications were adjusted, and life continued. He graduated high school at eighteen and got a job close to home.

Around that time, I had this wonderful, open and honest discussion with Christopher about drugs and alcohol. It was so much a two-way street of questions and answers that I felt comfortable enough to go on a fourteen day vacation, leaving Christopher at home to look after the pets. When I returned home a day early, I was horrified to find my living room and kitchen littered with drug paraphernalia, medication packets, and cannabis.

Christopher had become addicted to his ADHD medication and more. He was a high-functioning addict; his grades had been great on graduation, and a few short weeks before he was an employee of the month. No one knew he had a problem ... least of all me. It was off to rehabilitation. When he was discharged, I was hyper-vigilant for any sign of a relapse. I told him, 'one and done. I will not live with an addict under my roof.' He listened.

Life went on, and I thought all was well, but unbeknownst to me, Christopher had experienced workplace sexual harassment. When he told me, I encouraged and supported him in reporting this to human resources. His employer ignored it, so his anxiety increased, which caused extreme stress. This led to a catalyst of events - panic attacks and depression. He experienced an involuntary hospital stay, and doctors significantly increased his medication, leaving him unable to function upon release. He left the hospital with post-traumatic stress disorder (PTSD) as his sole souvenir. There were no follow-up arrangements to see a psychiatrist or psychologist, and I feel that Christopher was forgotten or lost in the system.

In 2020, Covid-19 happened, and anxiety, depression, and a diagnosis of bipolar was given. I think mental ill-health hid beside or behind Christopher's ADHD diagnosis. If it were in plain sight, I didn't see it. I must have been in denial, and I made excuses.

The reality of a bipolar diagnosis was new to me, so I shared with family and friends, hoping for love and perhaps the sharing of advice. This, however, was not the case. My only explanation is that I guess they don't know what to say. I questioned my relatives for hereditary links. Some were put off and nasty about it – again, shocking. All I wanted was a simple answer. I realised I was alone in this fight to help my child become stable and move forward. One friend I'd known for over forty years told me I was to never allow my son in my home again. That was the instant I chose to end our friendship.

Christopher's younger sister avoids him. My older children moved out of the house a number of years ago, and we are not super close, but we do talk occasionally.

What's the hospital system like in New Jersey?

The hospital system in the United States is awful. I have no rights as my child is over the age of eighteen. Hospital staff and health care workers would not speak to me, even with written waivers. After a second hospital stay, I got power of attorney for Christopher that included medical and mental illness. During his third emergency room stay, and after being involuntarily committed again (this time, it was very much needed), I showed them the power of attorney document and said I wanted a choice regarding where Christopher would be sent. Nope, it proved virtually worthless. Again, the system left me feeling helpless. We waited three weeks after my son's release to get a nurse practitioner's help with his medication. The nurse had voiced her concerns about the dosage of his medications, he was basically a zombie. Then a deep depression followed, and Christopher couldn't get out of bed for a week.

My experience of hospitals, well, so far, it's on the negative side. I've had to take Christopher to a mental health wellness hub twice. This is an emergency facility for mental health here in the United States. Unfortunately, this wasn't a positive experience either. At the time there wasn't a psychiatrist available on site, and so they weren't able to provide immediate assistance in reviewing his medication. In fact, we had to wait weeks after his discharge before being seen by a psychiatrist. Everything is wait and kick the can down the street.

Christopher finally got into therapy, and he has had two meetings, but now he has to wait two months for his next appointment. No reason has been given, perhaps there are just too many people in need of these services, and that in itself, is heart breaking. I'm angry at the hospital system, or lack of. We need to do better.

Maureen, are you silent about Christopher's mental health?

I am not silent. I have friends, but they are, for want of a better word, standoffish with this issue. So I'd rather not talk to them about it.

Have you read any helpful books or information?

I am reading many books about bipolar and anxiety to educate myself. I'm currently reading *Breaking Mad* by Anna Williamson, and I would recommend it. I also attend three different support groups to learn more about mental health concerns. I'm in touch with two different NAMI groups to educate myself about complex mental health concerns.

I've known for a while that I need to take care of myself. In the next few days, I will seek therapy. I'm still working on getting Christopher stable and taking one day at a time. We pray we are headed in the right direction, as three months have passed since his hospital stay. The process has been agonisingly slow. And this has taken a toll on me.

What do you do for you?

I have a wonderful fiancé. We've been together for fifteen years. I do lady brunches monthly and leave my worries behind for a little while. I often say to myself, 'I've got this! Better days ahead.' My tip for those reading this is never, ever lose hope.

Something I'd consider good for a caregiver is to go to a support group for the specific mental illness your loved one has. I go to a bipolar support group as a parent. Those that attend with lived experience are medicated, stable and doing really well. It gives me so much hope for my son and the future.

Lastly what would you tell your younger self that would help you now?

I would tell my younger self, 'Lady, you've got your shit together, but you have no clue how strong you truly are. You will amaze many, including yourself.'

Chapter 45
Trace's story living with anorexia nervosa

Sydney, Australia

> *Anorexia ruled my teenage years. It is not a subject I talk about anymore. I don't identify with that teenager who starved herself to near death.*
>
> — Trace

Trace and I met and bonded on a ward of a busy public hospital when we were nursing. I am grateful for the truth and vulnerability that she expressed. I wish I had known more about eating disorders back when we met, so I could have better helped my friend.

Can you remember when anorexia came into your life?

It was around 1977 when I noticed mental ill-health joining me at the table. I had been slim until puberty arrived, and then I gained weight ... or did I? I find it difficult to recall whether my memory is accurate.

A cheese commercial on TV featured the phrase 'round and mature, like me,' which a family friend repeated to me, and it stayed in my mind. It was the trigger that started the spiral. Magazines were full of diets. Our mothers ate diet biscuits to lose weight. The diet culture made eating less effortless. Friends also dieted, and then they stopped. I just didn't stop and then I didn't eat.

Some say anorexia is about control; I think at the time it was the only thing I had control of.

What were those early years like?

My local doctor picked up on my weight loss and referred me for help – which ended up being an admission to a hospital with ten other adolescents, all women. It wasn't long before I realised that this place, and the other patients, could give me more skills to cheat, lie, and manipulate my way out of any food put in front of me. I continued to spiral downwards for three years, then was hospitalised to put on weight. When I was discharged, my mission became to lose it all and more, only to be hospitalised again.

My parents were in charge of my care and followed instructions from the team looking after me. I went to a clinic in Sydney's northern suburbs where a specialised health care team looked after me; the goal being to see them as an outpatient.

Later, they hospitalised me. I was admitted to the adult psychiatric ward of a large Sydney public hospital because I wasn't responding to inpatient treatment at the clinic. I cannot explain the terror of being a young woman on a ward with men and women admitted with complex mental health conditions. After I was discharged from that place, I took part in an outpatient program for three years. Ultimately, I stopped going to the program as I wanted to put it all behind me. I did my best over the next few years, but occasionally slipped back into severe anorexic behaviours.

Dear Carer,

There were some wonderful doctors and psychologists, and it is great to see eating disorders supported by the Peter Beaumont Centre, especially with four percent of Australians, around one million people, living with an eating disorder. There were a couple of nurses who were supportive. I felt for the student nurses, as they were not that much older than me at the time. The program was hard, and they had to ensure we stuck to it. I would hope the programs have been refined now. It was a punishment and reward system. They may have been trying for a holistic approach, but I don't have those memories.

Anorexia ruled my teenage years. It is not a subject I talk about anymore. I don't identify with that teenager who starved herself to near death. My lowest point was when I weighed thirty-five kilograms and I was one hundred and seventy-two centimetres tall. Food, however, continued to rule my life. After a period of being overweight, I have spent my whole life trying to 'be the right weight'. I still control food by being the household cook, deciding what and where we eat. I am a body positive person now when it comes to size (though still self-critical of my own). I hate body shaming, and with a plus-size daughter, I am in awe of her beauty – it radiates with no bearing on her size.

Do you speak about anorexia nervosa to others?

I have spoken up when I have seen young people who appear anorexic. These have been confronting conversations, but I did my best to approach the matter gently. When I was diagnosed with an eating disorder, it was new to a lot of people. I lost friends, as they couldn't understand what I was doing. I have those friends back now, many years later, which is a wonderful gift

Trace, what do you do for yourself?

Self-care is such a new term, isn't it? It is a luxury I now can finally afford! I love facials, and I have been on trips just by myself to reset.

I'm happy to say my mental health is good. I have completed a mental health first aid certificate. Importantly, I understand who I am. But my health concerns have taken a big toll on my siblings and parents. I would still say it takes a toll on my ability to sustain a long-term relationship. Two failed marriages ...

People thrust books on me all the time. I have never found much value in self-help books. I *have* read books about my partner's daughter's psychiatric diagnosis to ensure that I can assist in any way possible.

Lastly – what would you tell your younger self that would help you now?

Remember that some may not understand, yet they'll still support you. You will live a long life, look for the things and people that make you happy. Trust in yourself and believe you are worth it.

Chapter 46
On Reflection

Reading these stories of lived experience may bring back memories or similarities for you. Each account has the same underlying current of guilt, stress, fatigue, silence, stigma - and hope. When I read through each story, I felt immense sadness that all felt unheard and unseen and the grief was sometimes palpable; it is part of the elastic that holds and bonds us together.

At the centre of each story is an unconditional love that has been tested in one of the hardest ways. Those living with complex mental health often cannot understand the why. The glue that holds life together can often be you, the carer. Thank you.

It was important for me to add Trace's story as someone with lived experience with complex mental health. To hear the complexities and reality of what she was living with.

Advocating for a loved one living with a chronic illness was likely not something that you planned to do. I call myself an accidental author because it was never something I thought I was capable of doing. I also call myself an accidental carer, because never in the realm of possibilities had I considered it.

There is no doubt in my mind that each and every wonderful human who has lived experience loving and caring for someone with complex mental health conditions is AMAZING.

Yes, that's *you*.

Chapter 47
Future Care

Future care to me means listening to those with lived experience. Utilising their knowledge to improve existing medical standards, procedures, government funding and grants.

— Sarah

Future care is building a sustainable workforce that has the skills, training and education needed to meet the future needs of all those that live with complex mental health conditions.

Future care is utilising trauma-informed care and recovery-oriented practice in the workplace, inpatient facilities, outpatient services and in the home, to guide and advocate for carers and loved ones alike. It is to listen to carers, their needs, their knowledge and to use this for the betterment of every person that comes under the mental health banner.

Future care means addressing the noticeable difference in accessing mental health services no matter where you live. Acknowledging that remote and rural communities suffer from a lack of infrastructure, ongoing education and mental health training.

Future care means listening to those with lived experience. Utilising their knowledge to improve existing medical standards, procedures, government funding and grants.

Future care is governments acknowledging and recognising the role that carers play in loving, living and looking after a loved one with needs, whether it be complex mental health or not.

Future care is governments budgeting for carers so that they can put food on the table and seek medical assistance for themselves AND their loved one.

Future care is speaking out about complex mental health concerns without fear of stigma.

Future care is breaking the silence of complex mental health so that we are all heard and seen.

How can we contribute to the mental health space in the future?

Many people want to know what they can do to bring about change. When one person believes in something passionately, I like to think that others join in. Positivity creates positivity. Like laughter, you just can't help but join in.

I recently took part in a mental health event organised by a group of university students. They invited celebrity chef Steph De Souza, who donated her time to do a segment on baking cookies. We all joined in preparing them online via Zoom. The comments in the chat were incredibly funny, flour was going everywhere, people dropped eggs and mixed up the order of ingredients, but it was genuine, wholesome fun. While the cookies were baking, Steph handed over to the students, who interviewed me (as a carer, writer, and nurse) and a young woman who was an honours student in psychology. Our conversation helped to break down those walls of silence, with others speaking out about their mental health for the first time. Baking and having a chat – it was inspiring in its simplicity. They also raised money for a mental health charity, which was the icing on the cookie! So yes, we can make change; it just needs the seed of an idea to make it happen.

Another positive step we can take is to write letters or emails to specific health ministers at state and national levels, asking for more government funding for mental health.

My vision is that in the future, upon arrival at an emergency department or psychiatric unit, a carer peer worker and a consumer peer worker[1] would greet you and your loved one in the hospital admissions area. They would accompany you and your loved one to the unit, then they or their team would be contactable throughout the admission. Imagine having someone there for you. To guide you through the mindfield of medical terminology, to alleviate a few of your fears and to hold space just for you and your loved ones.

Future care indeed.

Future care leads me onto the topic of hope

Hope, the Cambridge Dictionary states, is 'to want something to happen or to be true, and usually have a good reason to think it might'. We have all lived and breathed this word. Hope is what carers and those living with mental health concerns wish for and dream of.

It may come in the form of a morning spent in blissful silence as our loved one sleeps after a disrupted night. It may be a few minutes spent talking with our loved one about everything and nothing, but holding space in the now. It may be that moment your loved one smiles at you, not through you. It may be a shower and clean clothes. They all equal hope.

1. Mental health peer workers are trained professionals with lived experience who can support, guide and advocate for others who are going through similar things. A carer peer worker has lived experience of caring for someone with complex mental health concerns; a consumer peer worker has personal experience of living with complex mental health concerns.

My hope is that *Dear Carer,* has helped you, perhaps given you some direction or ideas of things to put in place, or ways to think differently over a situation. I hope that your friends read the 'Friend Care' chapter and gain insight into what you may be going through and what they can do to help. I hope that the health system gets easier to navigate for you and your loved one. I hope one day in the future that the stigma of mental health lessens ... I don't think I can say disappear because I'm not sure whether that is possible ... BUT nothing is impossible if we have hope.

On that note, my wish is that no one ever takes your hope away from you. It is yours to hold on to, no matter what.

To you, dear carer,
I hear your frustration, sadness, and grief.
I see your strength, power, resilience, and bravery.
With these, you are unstoppable; with knowledge, you are invincible.

Chapter 48
Information and Resource Care

Mental health platforms, forums and spaces

There are many mental health institutes, foundations, forums, spaces and mental health groups. I have assembled a few helpful resources – links will be in the 'Links to Resources' section following this chapter

It is impossible to include every mental health resource; this is a quick look for you to see what kinds of resources are available. Please be aware that any links posted may change - don't give up looking and asking questions because the link has changed.

The Australian Government Department of Health, Disability and Ageing

The Australian Government Department of Health, Disability and Ageing website is worth a look. Some of the topics covered include:

- Mental health and suicide prevention.
- Medicare mental health check in.

- Medicare for mental health.
- A collection of primary mental health care resources.
- Parents and carers.
- Carer Gateway.
- Support for carers.
- Young carers bursary program.

Each heading is full of information that can redirect you to valuable resources.

The Australian Psychological Society

This is an informative site on how to find a psychologist, with access to thousands of psychologists in Australia. Information on fees, types of psychologists and how a psychologist can help you.

Beyond Blue

A health organisation that provides:

- Free and confidential counselling.
- Free mental health coach for six sessions.
- Find a mental health professional (GPs. Psychologists. Psychiatrists. Mental health coaches. Social workers. Occupational therapists)
- Crisis Assessment or Acute Treatment Teams (otherwise known as CAT teams).
- First Nations Peoples and Torres Strait Islander health workers and support.
- Forums.
- Resources for carers or supporters.
- Counsellors.
- Men's health.

The Black Dog Institute

The Black Dog provides advice and analysis on mental health and suicide prevention. It has resources about suicide prevention and education so you can learn more and get support when you need it. You can read more about the history of the Black Dog Institute in the 'Medical Care Chapter' and find contact details in the 'Links to Resources' section at the end of the book.

Blue Knot Foundation

The Blue Knot Foundation's values are leading with hope, upholding integrity and driving change. The organisation's purpose is to empower people to recover from complex trauma and build resilience.

The organisation provides a safe space for survivors and those who support them. It provides a helpline, trauma counselling, and educational workshops, as well as a lot of resources and information. Blue Knot fosters a trauma-informed community in which lived experience matters, and in which everyone has a voice – a space that is inclusive, accepting, understanding and non-judgemental.

Carers Australia

Advocation is at the core of Carers Australia's primary objectives.

- Advocating and supporting policies and services that support carers.
- Developing and advocating for inclusivity within mainstream and individual programs.
- Improving outcomes for carers by acknowledging the shared responsibility from families to governments.
- Young carers network.
- Defence and veteran carers network.

- General information that includes links to other networks.
- National Disability Insurance Scheme (NDIS).
- Carer discounts and concessions.
- Centrelink payments for carers.

Full-time carers may be eligible for fortnightly carer payments.

- Income and asset tests.
- Must care for someone who meets the minimum disability score. This will need to be assessed by either a Carer's Needs Assessment or through the Adult Disability Assessment Tool.
- Must not work more than twenty five hours per week. Please check what forms of employment are allowed.
- Carers Allowance.
- Carers Supplement.
- Annual and one-off payments.

Links regarding government support will direct you from the Carers Australia site to Services Australia, where you will be required to sign in before starting the process to see if you are eligible for any of these payments. Remember if you don't ask, you don't receive.

Carer Gateway

I emailed Carer Gateway on a Friday afternoon. Within thirty minutes, a lovely lady returned my call. They work business hours, and she was concerned that if I had an urgent reason for contacting them, I would have to wait over the weekend to have my questions or concerns answered. That's a big tick from me.Importantly they offer help and support services for YOU.

Carer Gateway:

- Supports carers of someone who is frail, aged, has a disability, a chronic illness, or is in palliative care.
- Is a free national service funded by the Australian Government and accessible to all carers.
- Links carers with their peer support partners to help them connect with other carers in the area who may be going through similar situations.
- Offers other support services for carers, including free counselling, self-guided coaching online, skills courses online, emergency respite and short-term respite options.

A carer can call to register with Carer Gateway and will go through the intake process, which only takes a short time to complete. Once intake staff determine the caller's eligibility, they will get further details to decide what the next best course of action will be. If eligible, carers will be referred to a Carer Support Planner, who will look at each individual situation holistically to offer options and support to help carers in their caring role.

Headspace (for children, siblings and young adults)

A youth mental health foundation that provides early intervention, support, emergency assistance, and counselling services to twelve to twenty-five year olds, Australia wide. They will also support families and those caring for them.

They offer:

- Confidential and *free* chats with a trained clinician.
- Offer mentors, work and study support.
- Online community to connect and discuss resources.
- Information on mental health and online support.
- Walk-in Headspace centres are situated throughout Australia.

Legal Aid

In Australia, there are eight independent legal aid commissions that concentrate on making certain areas of law more accessible. For instance, Legal Aid in NSW has a translation service and offers different font sizes for those with visual impairments. Legal Aid offers:

- Family, friends and carer support.
- Accessible information.
- Mental health advocacy.
- Guardianship and financial management orders.
- Assistance in a courtroom.

Let's talk about voices

An initiative by Northern Sydney Local Health District in New South Wales that shares videos and worksheets about hearing voices. You can hear from others with lived experience and read their stories, so you know you are not alone.

Lifeline

For crisis support. Importantly, this service does not stop; it is 24/7 within Australia. You can also chat online, communicate face to face, text on your mobile, or call the number to talk with one of their trained volunteers. Their website states, 'they are shaping the way we talk about suicide.' The more we talk about mental health and suicide, the more we can break down the stigma.

MensLine

MensLine offers free assistance, referrals and counselling. It is a safe space for men to seek relationship advice, family violence education, programs and solutions.

- 24/7 phone counselling.
- Online chat line.
- Video chat.
- Free counselling and support

Mental Health Carers Australia

Mental Health Carers Australia (MHCA) are passionate advocates for carers. MHCA works with carers and supports those who cannot speak about what they and their loved ones are experiencing. They know that carers need to be able to share their stories and are compassionate listeners. Their actions and advocacy make it possible for us, as carers, to be seen and heard.

A key part of MHCA's work is building the capacity of families and carers to use their lived experience as lived expertise. This includes supporting carers in taking part in national advisory groups, government consultations and reform activities.

While MHCA does not provide direct services, it works closely with state and territory peak bodies and representative organisations that offer practical information and support for mental health carers. These include:

- Mental Health Carers NSW.
- Tandem Victoria.
- Arafmi Queensland.
- Mental Health Families and Friends Tasmania.
- Mental Health Carers Voice ACT.
- Helping Minds WA.

Each of these organisations provides advocacy, education and support that is tailored to local needs and service systems.

Mental health first aid courses

Mental Health First Aid International and Red Cross Australia offer mental health first aid courses. My wish and dream is that every workplace will make this course mandatory. There are many more courses online to choose from.

Roses in the Ocean

Its purpose is to save lives and reduce emotional stress and pain surrounding suicide. Their website has insightful information on lived experience with suicide and having someone call emergency services – look under 'Our 000 position'. More information about the organisation can be found in the chapter 'Suicide Care'.

SANE Australia

SANE is an organisation that assists people living with complex mental health conditions and concerns, those seeking advice regarding their own mental health, and their families, carers and friends. I am proud to be a SANE peer ambassador.

SANE offers forums, events, chat groups, and webinars. It also provides a national helpline that anyone can access, connecting people to services or informing them of available assistance.

SANE Support line – 1800 187 263. Available Monday to Friday from 10am – 8pm (AEST).

SANE Forums – peer to peer discussion, support, and webinars available 24/7 on all devices, moderated by mental health professionals. Features population-specific spaces including Yarning Space (for Aboriginal and/or Torres Strait Islander people) and Shoulder to Shoulder (for veterans and their families/carers).

SANE Recovery Club – a six month, self-paced online program providing access to mental health recovery planning resources and group support. Features weekly online recovery group calls with peer support.

SANE Guided Recovery – a fifteen week personalised recovery program providing 7 sessions with counselling or peer support for individuals and carers. Participants create personalised mental health recovery plans and participate in online recovery groups.

SANE Resources – SANE provides an extensive library of evidence-based fact sheets and guides to support people no matter where they are on their mental health journey. These include suicide prevention resources, downloadable fact sheets, lived experience stories, recovery tools and podcasts sharing stories of hope and recovery.

All SANE services and programs are accredited to the National Safety and Quality Digital Mental Health Standards.

Uniting

Uniting is a not-for-profit organisation that provides support, care, forums, respite, counselling, family services and more for carers and those they look after. They have information on a broad spectrum of services for our loved ones, including complex mental health concerns, seniors, disabilities, children, and families.

Their mission is to support families and carers and empower them in mental health recovery.

Their tagline is 'People are at the heart of what we do.'

If you are **not** *in Australia:*

Befrienders Worldwide.

Befrienders worldwide is a global suicide prevention charity.

Find a Helpline.

Find a Helpline provides a log of helplines from around the world that you can access.

National Alliance on Mental Illness (NAMI).

More commonly known by the acronym, NAMI provides support for those affected by mental ill-health in the United States.

National Health Service (NHS).

In the United Kingdom, the NHS is a major provider of support and information around mental health care.

References

Books

A Gut Mood Solution: A Groundbreaking Strategy for Managing Bipolar Disorders. *Professor Gordon Parker* (2025)

About a Girl: A Mother's Powerful Story of Raising Her Transgender Child. *Rebekah Robertson* (2019)

Bipolar II Disorder: Modelling, Measuring and Managing. *Professor Gordon Parker* (2008)

Brain Changer: How Diet Can Save Your Mental Health. P*rofessor Felice Jacka* (2019)

Breaking Mad: The Insider's Guide to Conquering Anxiety. *Anna Williamson* (2017)

Dear Psychosis, A story of hope and love through a family's journey of mental health. *Sarah Martin* (2023)

Different, Not Less: A Neurodivergent's Guide to Embracing Your True Self and Finding Your Happily Ever After. *Chloé Hayden* (2022)

How to Help Someone with Depression: A Practical Handbook. *Dr Emma Cotterill* (2021)

Hush: A Memoir Unravelling the Unintended Legacy of Family Secrets. *Michelle Scheibner* (2024)

Mental Health Microgains: 50 Small Actions That Will Make a Big Difference to Your Wellbeing. *Dr Tara Quinn-Cirillo & Dr Emma Cotterill* (2024)

Mental State: The Insanity of Australia's Mental Health System – and How to Fix It. *Dr Mark Cross* (2024)

Stop Worrying About Your Money. *Jacqui Clarke* (2023)

Sarah Martin

Spiritual Emergency: When Personal Transformation Becomes a Crisis. *Stanislav Grof & Christina Grof* (1989)

The Devil You Knew: The Power of Being Honest About Mental Illness. *Professor Ian Hickie* (2023)

The Five Love Languages: How to Express Heartfelt Commitment to Your Mate. *Gary Chapman* (1992)

The Myth of Normal: Trauma, Illness, and Healing in a Toxic Culture. *Gabor Maté (with Daniel Maté)* (2022)

Mental Health Resources

Please be aware that any links posted may change - don't give up looking and asking questions because the link has changed.

Australia

ACAP Psychology Clinic.

Https://www.acap.edu.au/applied-psychology/psychology/psychology-clinic/

Alcohol and Drug Foundation.

https://adf.org.au

Alcohol and Drug Foundation Hotline: 1800 250 015

Arafmi Queensland.

https://arafmi.com.au/

Australian Government – Department of Health, Disability and Ageing.

https://www.health.gov.au
https://www.health.gov.au/node/44804?query=mental+health

The Australian Psychological Society.

https://psychology.org.au/

Befrienders Worldwide (Global Suicide Prevention)

https://www.befrienders.org

Beyond Blue

https://www.beyondblue.org.au
Counselling: 1300 224 636 or online chat

Black Dog Institute

https://www.blackdoginstitute.org.au

Blue Knot Foundation

https://www.blueknot.org.au

Carers Australia

https://www.carersaustralia.com.au

Carer Gateway

https://www.carergateway.gov.au

EPIC – Empowering Parents in Crisis

https://www.empoweringparentsincrisis.com

Find a Helpline (international support when away from home)

https://findahelpline.com

Food & Mood Centre

https://foodandmoodcentre.com.au/smiles-trial

Griefline

https://www.griefline.org.au

Headspace

https://headspace.org.au
Phone: 1800 650 890

Helping Minds WA

https://helpingminds.org.au/

Legal Aid – Australia

Legal Aid ACT – https://www.legalaidact.org.au

Legal Aid New South Wales – https://www.legalaid.nsw.gov.au
Legal Services Commission of South Australia – https://lsc.sa.gov.au
Legal Aid Queensland – https://www.legalaid.qld.gov.au
Legal Aid Tasmania – https://www.legalaid.tas.gov.au
Legal Aid Victoria – https://www.legalaid.vic.gov.au
Legal Aid Western Australia – https://www.legalaid.wa.gov.au
National Legal Aid – https://nationallegalaid.org.au

Let's Talk About Voices (NSW Health)

https://www.nslhd.health.nsw.gov.au/hearingvoices/Pages/default.aspx

Lifeline

https://www.lifeline.org.au
Call: 13 11 14
Text: 0477 13 11 14

MensLine Australia

https://mensline.org.au
Call: 1300 789 978

Mental Health Acts (by State)

ACT – https://www.act.gov.au/health/mental-health-care/mental-health-care-and-your-rights/about-the-mental-health-act

NSW – https://legislation.nsw.gov.au/view/whole/html/inforce/current/act-2007-008
Queensland – https://www.health.qld.gov.au/public-health/topics/mhaod/legislation-and-courts/mental-health-law-and-courts/about-the-mental-health-act-2016
South Australia – https://www.sahealth.sa.gov.au/wps/wcm/connect/public+content/sa+health+internet/about+us/legislation/mental+health+act+2009
Tasmania – https://www.legislation.tas.gov.au/view/whole/html/inforce/current/act-2013-002
Western Australia – https://www.legislation.wa.gov.au/legislation/statutes.nsf/main_mrtitle_13534_homepage.html
Victoria – https://www.legislation.vic.gov.au/as-made/acts/mental-health-and-wellbeing-act-2022

Mental Health Carers Australia

https://www.mentalhealthcarersaustralia.org.au

Mental Health Carers Voice ACT

https://mhcv.org.au/

Mental Health First Aid Training

https://www.mhfa.com.au
https://firstaid.redcross.org.au/mental-health-first-aid/

Mental Health Families and Friends Tasmania

https://tasmanconnect.org.au/service-directory/mental-health/mental-health-families-friends-tasmania/

Mental Health Rights Manual

https://mhrm.mhcc.org.au

National Debt Helpline

https://ndh.org.au

Roses in the Ocean

https://rosesintheocean.com.au/

SANE Australia

https://www.sane.org

Services Australia

https://www.servicesaustralia.gov.au

Suicide Call Back Service

Phone: 1300 659 467

Tandem Victoria

https://www.tandemcarers.org.au/

Uniting

https://www.uniting.org/home

International Resources

Canada

Canadian Mental Health Association

https://cmha.ca

New Zealand

Mental Health Foundation

https://mentalhealth.org.nz

United Kingdom

Mind

https://www.mind.org.uk

NHS – Mental Health

https://www.nhs.uk/mental-health/

United States

NAMI

https://www.nami.org

Professional Links

Sarah Martin

Website: https://sarahmartinauthor.com
Instagram: https://www.instagram.com/sarahmartin.author/
LinkedIn: https://www.linkedin.com/in/sarah-martin123/
Facebook: https://www.facebook.com/profile.php?id=
100088825839661

Dr Amanda Ferguson

Website: https://www.dramandaferguson.com.au
LinkedIn: https://www.linkedin.com/in/dramandaferguson/
Instagram: https://www.instagram.com/dramandaferguson/
Facebook: https://www.facebook.com/doctoramandaferguson

Jacqui Clarke

https://www.jacquiclarke.me
Instagram: https://www.instagram.com/jacquiclarke00/

Acknowledgments

THANK YOU

When a child skips beside you, jumps in mud puddles and gets soaked by the rain, you know that they are at their happiest. This is how I have felt writing *Dear Carer,*

Don't get me wrong, there have been days I have been on the edge of frustration, only to wake up in bed and know what the solution is. I have been talking to colleagues and stopped mid-chat because the perfect sentence has formed in my brain. On the flip side, I have held the right words gently in my hands, only for them to flitter away like butterflies.

The words came. New chapters formed.

Then, a wonderful thing happened. People heard I was writing a book for carers and asked if they could share their lived or professional expertise.

I started skipping.

Our daughter lives with bipolar I. She has fought the war with psychosis, depression, and anxiety. To her I say:

> I know some, but not all the battles you fight. I see, but cannot feel, the myriad of invisible, silent scars that you live with. We are proud of your resilience. We are proud of your strength. We are proud of who you are. Thank you for being our daughter.

To my family and friends who have listened to me talk constantly about *Dear Carer,* thank you for holding space for me.

To my carer friends – and there are many. Thank you for allowing me to be a part of your lives, for sharing your wisdom and strength. Most of all, thank you for showing me the power of advocacy and perseverance.

To everyone who has contributed to these pages with their knowledge, power, information and wisdom, I thank you.

My husband, Shane, for being my pillar of strength and my grammatical guru ... again. But mostly for believing in me and being my number one, my love and my very best friend.

My kids. Indulge me while I share some proud mumma moments!

Jesse, an amazing doctor whose wisdom and knowledge are inspiring. He has been our wise child, with words to ease us and knowledge to ground us when we could not find answers. A budding author, I cannot wait to see his books in print and racing off the shelves. He weaves pictures and words together like no one I have read before. His sidekick in life, E, is one of the kindest, most gentle of humans to walk the earth. Her calmness creates a peaceful space that is bound in love.

Our darling Alice has navigated a path that we could never have imagined, but one that she knew was hers. She completed her university studies in 2015, before the tentacles of mental ill-health wrapped tightly around her.

She is currently earning further degrees in the mental health space so she can share her knowledge and assist those with similar lived experience and more.

Shane and I are so proud of all you have done and will achieve in the future.

To her partner, K, whose gentle heart defies his towering height, thank you for loving and cherishing our girl.

Delightful Harry is our youngest. As a thirteen-year-old living with a sister with complex mental health concerns, we worried that he would be exposed to hard truths and the harshness of life. But each day he brought positivity home. He nurtured us when we needed it the most, and we are the proudest of parents watching him complete his paramedicine degree. He will have lived experience of mental ill-health, and I know that his kindness and strength will help many in the years to come. To his partner, B, the peace we feel when you walk into the room is instantaneous.

My wonderful sister, best friend and sounding board, Jane. The support you give has no boundaries.

My writing buddies and fellow authors, Melissa Le Mesurier, Melinda Charlesworth, and Maggie Walters, who continue to offer support, strength, and wisdom, with a no-BS attitude to go with it. Your mentorship and encouragement is invaluable, but it's the friendship we have made that will last a lifetime.

Their books may be on the shelves now, so give them a google.

Dear Carer, could not exist without the amazing people who shared articles, information, knowledge, and experience, whether through their professional lives or lived experience.

Thankyou from my heart to yours.

Every single carer and every single loved one who lives with complex mental health concerns, I see you and I hear you.

Professor Gordon Parker AO for his wise words and friendship.

Dr Amanda Ferguson. Jacqui Clarke.

Kirsty, Anu and Emily, in fact, the entire team from SANE Australia.

Tracey, Lindsay, Alex and Mel, Kathy, Claire, Maureen, Christopher, Rita, Portia, Lyndal, Georgie and Fi.

Megan, Jes, Stacey Leigh, Cassie and Lauren, Linda C and Eric B (thanks for forwarding to the boss)

My runaways, Shaunaugh and Donna, for always keeping it real.

My beta readers, who have made *Dear Carer,* better with their insights and to whom I am so incredibly grateful: Mel, Matt, Liz and Claire.

Cristie, who has the kindness, heart and strength of a village, thank you for your unwavering support and friendship, and Reggie for being her rock.

Hazel Lam, cover designer. WOW! Thank you for saying yes.

Lu Sexton who appraised an early version of *Dear Carer,*

Kathryn Tafra, who has been amazing as my editor extraordinaire, thank you.

Alex Watson for doing an in-depth, no word left unturned proofread. Seriously brilliant.

Christopher Brennan for indexing and teaching me a lot about something I didn't know!

Melinda Charlesworth for formatting Dear Carer, to absolute perfection.

My fellow carer peer workers who let me inundate them with questions and cheered this book on every step of the way. Eileen, the two Peter H's, Simon and Lyn.

My dad, Papa, and my beautiful mum, Juju – who may not be with us but is definitely here in spirit (the FOMO was strong with Mum). And my brothers, Matt and David, and sister Jane (yes you can have two mentions) – the bonds between us have strengthened more as the years go by, of which I am grateful.

To all those at work in the operating theatres at NSSDH. Thank you for being my captive audience and letting me talk all things mental health (nothing like being in an operating theatre with no escape except for breaks. BEST crowd EVER.): Kerrie, Maria, Pip, Briggie, Josephine, Gracie, Ellen, Philomena, Liz, Georgia, Michelle, Harry, Eleanor, Sophia, Adele and Hilary.

And to my friends near and far who encourage me by asking questions and showing interest in mental health.

To others that may have slipped my mind to thank here, please know that you are not forgotten, and your input was genuinely appreciated ... forgive a seniors moment on my part.

Last, 'last words' from me

If you've made it this far, don't stop now.

Come visit me on my Instagram (@sarahmartin.author) where we can continue the conversation, as I will never, ever, stop advocating for mental health.

I love speaking out about being a carer and breaking the stigma and silence around complex mental health concerns. If you'd like to have me talk at your work or conference, please contact me via my author website.

Don't forget to pop a review wherever you leave your book reviews because that is a wonderful way to share *Dear Carer,* and spread the word.

Oh, and tell your local library to get our books in, so others can read them too.

I have taken the liberty to write a teeny tiny toolkit book, with a list of all or most of the ideas and strategies I have mentioned in Dear Carer, to try and make life a little easier for you.

If you'd like to look at it, head to my website.

It will be in two forms.

Notebook and pdf.

I am more of a notebook, pen and paper lady but I know many aren't – so you can choose.

Please don't hesitate to contact me at https://sarahmartinauthor.com

Index

. . .

. . .